The Little LISPer
Third Edition

The Little LISPer
Third Edition

Daniel P. Friedman

Indiana University
Bloomington, Indiana

Matthias Felleisen

Rice University
Houston, Texas

Foreword by Gerald J. Sussman

Cover Illustration by Guy L. Steele Jr.

Macmillan Publishing Company
New York

Collier Macmillan Publishers
London

Macmillan Publishing Company
866 Third Avenue, New York, New York 10022

Collier Macmillan Canada, Inc.

Printed in the United States of America

Library of Congress Cataloging-in-Publication Data

Friedman, Daniel P.
   The little LISPer / Daniel P. Friedman, Matthias Felleisen;
foreword for Gerald J. Sussman; cover illustrations by Guy L.
Steele, Jr. — 3rd ed.
      p. cm.
   Includes index.
   ISBN 0-02-339763-2
   1. LISP (Computer program language)   I. Felleisen, Matthias.
II. Title.
QA76.73.L23F74   1989   88-38980
005.13′3—dc19   CIP

Printing: 2 3 4 5 6 7 8 9 10   Year: 9 0 1 2 3 4 5

To Mary and Helga,
to our sons
Brian, Robert, and Christopher,
and to the memory of Elliott I. Organick

(Contents

)

Foreword

In 1967 I took an introductory course in photography. Most of the students (including me) came into that course hoping to learn how to be creative—to take pictures like the ones I admired by artists such as Edward Weston. On the first day the teacher patiently explained the long list of technical skills that he was going to teach us during the term. A key was Ansel Adams' "Zone System" for previsualizing the print values (blackness in the final print) in a photograph and how they derive from the light intensities in the scene. In support of this skill we had to learn the use of exposure meters to measure light intensities and the use of exposure time and development time to control the black level and the contrast in the image. This is in turn supported by even lower level skills such as loading film, developing and printing, and mixing chemicals. One must learn to ritualize the process of developing sensitive material so that one gets consistent results over many years of work. The first laboratory session was devoted to finding out that developer feels slippery and that fixer smells awful.

But what about creative composition? In order to be creative one must first gain control of the medium. One can not even begin to think about organizing a great photograph without having the skills to make it happen. In engineering, as in other creative arts, we must learn to do analysis to support our efforts in synthesis. One cannot build a beautiful and functional bridge without a knowledge of steel and dirt and considerable mathematical technique for using this knowledge to compute the properties of structures. Similarly, one cannot build a beautiful computer system without a deep understanding of how to "previsualize" the process generated by the procedures one writes.

Some photographers choose to use black-and-white 8×10 plates while others choose 35mm slides. Each has its advantages and disadvantages. Like photography, programming requires a choice of medium. Lisp is the medium of choice for people who enjoy free style and flexibility. Lisp was initially conceived as a theoretical vehicle for recursion theory and for symbolic algebra. It has developed into a uniquely powerful and flexible family of software development tools, providing wrap-around support for the rapid-prototyping of software systems. As with other languages, Lisp provides the glue for using a vast library of canned parts, produced by members of the user community. In Lisp, procedures are first-class data, to be passed as arguments, returned as values, and stored in data structures. This flexibility is valuable, but most importantly, it provides mechanisms for formalizing, naming, and saving the idioms—the common patterns of usage that are essential to engineering design. In addition, Lisp programs can easily manipulate the representations of Lisp programs—a feature that has encouraged the development of a vast structure of program synthesis and analysis tools, such as cross-referencers.

The Little LISPer is a unique approach to developing the skills underlying creative programming in Lisp. It painlessly packages, with considerable wit, much of the drill and practice that is necessary to learn the skills of constructing recursive processes and manipulating recursive data-structures. For the student of Lisp programming, *The Little LISPer* can perform the same service that Hanon's finger exercises or Czerny's piano studies perform for the student of piano.

Gerald J. Sussman
Cambridge, Massachusetts

Preface

Recursion is the act of defining an object or solving a problem in terms of itself. A careless recursion can lead to an infinite regress. We avoid the bottomless circularity inherent in this tactic by demanding that the recursion be stated in terms of some "simpler" object, and by providing the definition or solution of some trivial base case. Properly used, recursion is a powerful problem solving technique, both in artificial domains like mathematics and computer programming, and in real life.

The goal of this book is to teach the reader to think recursively. Our first task, therefore, is to decide which language to use to communicate this concept. There are three obvious choices: a natural language, such as English; formal mathematics; or a programming language. Natural languages are ambiguous, imprecise, and sometimes awkwardly verbose. These are all virtues for general communication, but something of a drawback for communicating concisely as precise a concept as the power of recursion. The language of mathematics is the opposite of natural language: it can express powerful formal ideas with only a few symbols. We could, for example, describe the entire technical content of this book in less than a page of mathematics, but the reader who understands that page has little need for this book. For most people, formal mathematics is not very intuitive. The marriage of technology and mathematics presents us with a third, almost ideal choice: a programming language. Programming languages are perhaps the best way to convey the concept of recursion. They share with mathematics the ability to give a formal meaning to a set of symbols. But unlike mathematics, programming languages can be directly experienced—you can take the programs in this book and try them, observe their behavior, modify them, and experience the effect of your modifications.

Perhaps the best programming language for teaching recursion is Lisp. Lisp is inherently symbolic—the programmer does not have to make an explicit mapping between the symbols of his own language and the representations in the computer. Recursion is Lisp's natural computational mechanism; the primary programming activity is the creation of (potentially) recursive definitions. Lisp implementations are predominantly interactive—the programmer can immediately participate in and observe the behavior of his programs. And, perhaps most importantly for our lessons at the end of this book, there is a direct correspondence between the structure of Lisp programs and the data those programs manipulate.

Lisp is practical. It is the dominant language for work in artificial intelligence: computational linguistics, robotics, pattern recognition, expert systems, generalized problem solving, theorem proving, game playing, algebraic manipulation, etc. It has had a major influence on most other fields of computer science.

Although Lisp can be described quite formally, understanding Lisp does not require a particularly mathematical inclination. In fact, *The Little LISPer* is based on lecture notes from a two-week "quickie" introduction to Lisp for students with no previous programming experience and an admitted dislike for anything quantitative. Many of these students were preparing for careers in public affairs. It is our belief that *writing programs recursively in Lisp is essentially simple pattern recognition.* Since our only concern is recursive programming, our treatment is limited to the why's and wherefore's of just a few Lisp features: car, cdr, cons, eq?, atom?, null?, number?, zero?, add1, sub1, not, and, or, quote, lambda, define, and cond. Indeed, our language is an *idealized* Lisp.

The Little LISPer is not a complete book on Lisp. However, mastery of the concepts in this book is mastery of the foundations of Lisp—after you understand this material, the rest will be easy.

Acknowledgements

Many people made important contributions to the first edition of this book. The following acknowledgement appeared there:

Many thanks to John McCarthy, Mike Greenawalt, John Howard, Terry Pratt, David Musser, William Gear, Mark Elson, Harold Stone, Jonathan Slocum, Juny Armus, Bob Wesson, and Marylin Sealy for their extremely helpful comments about *The Little LISPer*. Grateful appreciation to Ben Shneiderman and Steve Mitchell for believing in this unorthodox approach to Lisp. Thank you to Bill Cohagan who taught me Lisp and to Ann and Frances Patterson for their careful typing and proofreading of this manuscript. I am greatly indebted to Patrick Mahaffey for his futuristic ideas of teaching Lisp to public affairs graduate students and to John Gronouski, Dean of the Lyndon Baines Johnson School of Public Affairs, who was persuaded to try the experiment. I want to thank the four public affairs graduate students, Phillip S. Blackerby, Robert J. King, David L. Walrath, and Abraham Goldberg who not only were students in the "quickie" course but also persevered with me an additional week for the completion of the first draft. I especially want to thank Abraham Goldberg who contributed his editing talents and novice perspective for that week. Above all, I want to thank my wife Mary for her understanding, encouragement, and concern for my well-being during the completion of this manuscript.

We are indebted to many people for their contributions and assistance throughout the development of this book. We thank Bruce Duba, Kent Dybvig, Chris Haynes, Eugene Kohlbecker, Richard Salter, George Springer, Mitch Wand, and David S. Wise for countless discussions which influenced our thinking while conceiving this book. Ghassan Abbas, Charles Baker, David Boyer, Mike Dunn, Terry Falkenberg, Robert Friedman, John Gateley, Mayer Goldberg, Iqbal Khan, Julia Lawall, Jon Mendelsohn, John Nienart, Jeffrey D. Perotti, Ed Robertson,

Anne Shpuntoff, Erich Smythe, Guy Steele, Todd Stein, and Larry Weisselberg provided many important comments on the drafts of the book. We especially want to thank Bob Filman for being such a thorough and uncompromising critic through several readings. Finally we wish to acknowledge Nancy Garrett, Peg Fletcher, and Bob Filman for contributing to the design and TEXery. We particularly want to thank Nancy for her valiant efforts in correcting errors and entering changes in what must have seemed a sea of incomprehensible ASCII.

Guidelines for the Reader

Do not rush through this book. Read carefully; valuable hints are scattered throughout the text. Do not read the book in less than three sittings unless you are already familiar with Lisp but are not a "LISPer." Read systematically. If you do not *fully* understand one chapter, you will understand the next one even less. The questions are ordered by increasing difficulty; it will be hard to answer later ones if you cannot solve the earlier ones.

Guess! This book is based on intuition, and yours is as good as anyone's. Also, if you can, try the examples while you read. Lisps are readily available. While there are minor syntactic variations between different implementations of Lisp (primarily the spelling of particular names and the domain of specific functions), Lisp is basically the same throughout the world. To work with Lisp, you may need to modify the programs slightly. Typically, the material requires only a few changes for modern Lisps such as COMMON LISP [4] and Scheme [1, 2]. Suggestions about how to try the programs in the book are provided in the footnotes. Footnotes preceded by "L:" concern Lisp, those by "S:" concern Scheme. For Scheme, you may have to enter the definitions of add1, sub1, and atom? because some implementations do not provide these functions:

```
(define add1 (let ((f +)) (lambda (x) (f x 1))))
(define sub1 (let ((f -)) (lambda (x) (f x 1))))
(define atom? (let ((f1 pair?) (f2 not)) (lambda (x) (f2 (f1 x)))))
```

We have formulated these definitions in such way that they are safe from re-definition of built-in functions; this is particularly important for Chapter 4 where we discuss versions of + and - in terms of add1 and sub1.

We do not give any formal definitions in this book. We believe that you can form your own definitions and will thus remember them and understand them better than if we had written each one for you. But be sure you know and understand the *Laws* and *Commandments* thoroughly before passing them by. The key to learning Lisp is "pattern recognition." The *Commandments* point out the patterns that you will have already seen. Early in the book, some concepts are narrowed for simplicity; later, they are expanded and qualified. You should also know that, while everything in the book is Lisp, Lisp itself is more general and incorporates more than we could intelligibly cover in an introductory text. After you have mastered this book, you can read and understand more advanced and comprehensive books on Lisp.

We use a few notational conventions throughout the text, primarily changes in font for different classes of symbols. Programs in notes preceded by "L:" or "S:" are set in **typewriter font**. Function definitions are in roman characters, parameters are in *italic*, and data is in sans serif. The values for true and false are in *slanted font*. Special symbols such as **define** and **cond** are in **boldface**. These distinctions can be safely ignored until Chapter 10, when we treat programs as data. We have taken certain liberties with punctuation to increase clarity.

Food appears in many of our examples for two reasons. First, food is easier to visualize than abstract symbols. (This is not a good book to read while dieting.) We hope the choice of food will help you understand the examples and concepts we use. Second, we want to provide you with a little distraction. We know how frustrating the subject matter can be, and a little distraction will help you keep your sanity.

You are now ready to start. Good luck! We hope you will enjoy the challenges waiting for you on the following pages.

Bon appétit!

Daniel P. Friedman
Matthias Felleisen
Bloomington, Indiana

About the cover

RECURSION: YIN AND LANGDA

The ancient and
beautiful Chinese yin-yang
symbol represents complementary
but harmonious principles (such as earth
and heaven, female and male, dark and light)
that make up all aspects of life and the universe.
In modified form it illustrates the complementary
but harmonious relationship between two important theories of recursive functions: the combinatory
calculus and the lambda calculus. Each separately
is computationally universal, but the combinatory
calculus has no variables while the very essence of
the lambda calculus (on which Lisp is based) is
the correct treatment of bound variables—yet
the two calculi can be integrated smoothly.
By a curious coincidence, the symbols
most representative of the two calculi, Y and λ, are related by
a 180° rotation.

Illustration and commentary by Guy L. Steele Jr.

Chapter 1

Toys

Is it true that this is an *atom*?
  atom[1]
	Yes,
	    because atom is a string of characters beginning with the letter a.

[1] L,S: (quote atom) or 'atom
"L:" and "S:" are described on page xiii.

Is it true that this is an atom?
  turkey
	Yes,
	    because turkey is a string of characters beginning with a letter.

Is it true that this is an atom?
  1492
	Yes,
	    since 1492 is a string of characters beginning with a digit.

Is it true that this is an atom?
  3turkeys
	Yes,
	    since 3turkeys is a string of characters beginning with a digit.

Is it true that this is an atom?
  u
	Yes,
	    because u is a string of one character beginning with a letter or digit.

Is it true that this is an atom?
  *abc$
	Yes,
	    because *abc$ is a string of characters beginning with a letter, digit, or special character other than a left "(" or right ")" parenthesis.

Is it true that this is a *list*?
  (atom)[1]
	Yes,
	    because (atom) is an atom enclosed by parentheses.

[1] L,S: (quote (atom)) or '(atom)

Is it true that this is a list?
  (atom turkey or)
	Yes,
	    because it is a collection of atoms enclosed by parentheses.

Is it true that this is a list?
  (atom turkey) or
	No,
	    since this is actually two *S-expressions* not enclosed by parentheses. The first one is a list containing two atoms, and the second one is an atom.

Is it true that this is a list?
  ((atom turkey) or)
	Yes,
	    because the two S-expressions are now enclosed by parentheses.

Is it true that this is an S-expression?
  xyz
	Yes,
	    because all atoms are S-expressions.

Is it true that this is an S-expression?
  (x y z)
	Yes,
	    because it is a list.

Is it true that this is an S-expression?
  ((x y) z)
	Yes,
	    because all lists are S-expressions.

Is it true that this is a list?
  (how are you doing so far)
	Yes,
	    because it is a collection of S-expressions enclosed by parentheses.

How many S-expressions are in the list
  (how are you doing so far)
and what are they?
	Six,
	    how, are, you, doing, so, and far.

Is it true that this is a list?
   (((how) are) ((you) (doing so)) far)
	Yes,
	   because it is a collection of S-expressions enclosed by parentheses.

How many S-expressions are in the list
   (((how) are) ((you) (doing so)) far)
and what are they?
	Three,
	   ((how) are), ((you) (doing so)), and far.

Is it true that this is a list?
   ( )
	Yes,
	   because it contains zero S-expressions enclosed by parentheses. This special S-expression is called the *null list*.

Is it true that this is an atom?
   ( )
	Yes,
	   because ( ) is both a list and an atom.

Is it true that this is a list?
   (( ) ( ) ( ) ( ))
	Yes,
	   because it is a collection of S-expressions enclosed by parentheses.

What is the *car* of l, where l is the *argument*
   (a b c)
	a,
	   because a is the first atom of this list.

What is the car of l, where l is the argument
   ((a b c) x y z)
	(a b c),
	   because (a b c) is the first S-expression of this non-null list.

What is the car of l, where l is the argument
   hotdog
	No answer.
	   You cannot ask for the car of an atom.

What is the car of *l*, where *l* is the argument
  ( )
	No answer.[1]
	  You cannot ask for the car of an atom.

---
[1] L: nil

The Law of Car

Car is defined only for non-null lists.

What is the car of *l*, where *l* is the argument
  (((hotdogs)) (and) (pickle) relish)
	((hotdogs)).
	  Read as:
	    "The list of the list of hotdogs."
	  ((hotdogs)) is the first S-expression of *l*.

What is (car *l*), where *l* is the argument
  (((hotdogs)) (and) (pickle) relish)
	((hotdogs)),
	  because (car *l*) is another way to ask for
	  "the car of the list *l*."

What is (car (car *l*)), where *l* is the argument (((hotdogs)) (and))	(hotdogs).

What is the *cdr* of *l*, where *l* is the argument
  (a b c)
 	
Note: "cdr" is pronounced "could-er."
	(b c),
	  because (b c) is the list *l*, without (car *l*).

What is the cdr of *l*, where *l* is the argument ((a b c) x y z)	(x y z).

What is (cdr *l*), where *l* is the argument
    ((x) t r)
	(t r),
	    because (cdr *l*) is just another way to ask
	    for "the cdr of the list *l*."

What is (cdr *a*), where *a* is the argument
    hotdogs
	No answer.
	    You cannot ask for the cdr of an atom.

What is (cdr *l*), where *l* is the argument
    ( )
	No answer.[1]
	    You cannot ask for the cdr of the null list.

---
[1] L: nil

The Law of Cdr

Cdr is defined only for non-null lists. The cdr of any non-null list is always another list.

What is (car (cdr *l*)), where *l* is the argument
    ((b) (x y) ((c)))
	(x y),
	    because ((x y) ((c))) is (cdr *l*), and (x y) is
	    the car of (cdr *l*).

What is (cdr (cdr *l*)), where *l* is the argument
    ((b) (x y) ((c)))
	(((c))),
	    because ((x y) ((c))) is (cdr *l*), and (((c)))
	    is the cdr of (cdr *l*).

What is (cdr (car *l*)), where *l* is the argument
    (a (b (c)) d)
	No answer,
	    since (car *l*) is an atom, and cdr does not
	    take an atom for an argument; see The
	    Law of Cdr.

What does car take as an argument?	It takes any non-null list as its argument.
What does cdr take as an argument?	It takes any non-null list as its argument.

What is the *cons* of the atom *a* and the list *l*, where
    a is the argument peanut, and
    l is the argument (butter and jelly)
This can also be written "(cons *a l*)."
    Read: "cons the atom *a* onto the list *l*."
	(peanut butter and jelly),
	    because cons adds an atom to the front of a list.

What is the cons of *s* and *l*, where
    s is (mayonnaise and), and
    l is (peanut butter and jelly)
	((mayonnaise and) peanut butter and jelly),
	    because cons adds any S-expression to the front of a list.

What is (cons *s l*), where
    s is ((help) this), and
    l is (is very ((hard) to learn))
	(((help) this) is very ((hard) to learn)).

What does cons take as its arguments?	cons takes two arguments:
	    the first one is any S-expression;
	    the second one is any list.

What is (cons *s l*), where
    s is (a b (c)), and
    l is ( )
	((a b (c))),
	    because ( ) is a list.

What is (cons *s l*), where
    s is a, and
    l is ( )
	(a).

What is (cons *s* *l*), where
  s is (a b (c)), and
  l is b
	No answer,[1]
	  since the second argument *l must* be a list.

---

[1] In practice, (cons α β), where α and β are any entities, works. Then, if γ is (cons α β), (car γ) is α, (cdr γ) is β, and (cons (car γ) (cdr γ)) = γ.

What is (cons *s* *l*), where
  s is a, and
  l is b
	No answer.
	  Why?

The Law of Cons

Cons takes two arguments. The second argument of cons must be a list. The result is a list.

What is (cons *s* (car *l*)), where
  s is a, and
  l is ((b) c d)
	(a b).
	  Why?

What is (cons *s* (cdr *l*)), where
  s is a, and
  l is ((b) c d)
	(a c d).
	  Why?

Is it true that the list *l* is the null list, where
  l is ( )
This question can also be written:
  (null? *l*)
	Yes,
	  because it is the list composed of zero
	  S-expressions.

What is (null?[1] (**quote** ( )))	True, because (**quote** ( ))[1] is a way of expressing the null list.

<hr>

[1]   L: null

[1]   L: ()
    S: '()

Is (null? *l*) true or false, where *l* is the argument (a b c)	False, because it is a non-null list.

Is (null? *a*) true or false, where *a* is spaghetti	No answer,[1] because you cannot ask null? of a non-null atom.

[1]   In practice, (null? *a*), where *a* is an atom, is well defined. The beginner should follow The Law of Null?

> # The Law of Null?
>
> ### Null? is defined only for lists.

Is it true or false, that *s* is an atom, where *s* is Harry	True, because Harry is a string of characters beginning with a letter.

Is (atom?[1] *s*) true or false, where *s* is Harry	True, because (atom? *s*) is just another way to ask, "Is it true or false that *s* is an atom?"

[1]   L: atom
    S: See Preface, page xiii.

Is (atom? *s*) true or false, where
    s is (Harry had a heap of apples)
	False,
	    since the argument *s* is a list.

How many arguments does atom? take, and what are they?	It takes *one* argument. The argument can be any S-expression.

Is (atom? (car *l*)) true or false, where
    l is (Harry had a heap of apples)
	True,
	    because (car *l*) is Harry, and Harry is an atom.

Is (atom? (cdr *l*)) true or false, where *l* is (Harry had a heap of apples)	False.

Is (atom? (cdr *l*)) true or false, where
    l is (Harry)
	True,
	    because the list ( ) is also an atom.

Is (atom? (car (cdr *l*))) true or false, where
    l is (swing low sweet cherry)
	True,
	    because (cdr *l*) is (low sweet cherry), and (car (cdr *l*)) is low, which is an atom.

Is (atom? (car (cdr *l*))) true or false, where
    l is (swing (low sweet) cherry)
	False,
	    since (cdr *l*) is ((low sweet) cherry), and (car (cdr *l*)) is (low sweet), which is a list.

True or false: *a1* and *a2* are the same atom, where
    a1 is Harry, and
    a2 is Harry
	True,
	    because *a1* is the atom Harry and *a2* is the atom Harry.

Is (eq?[1] *a1* *a2*) true or false, where
   a1 is the argument Harry, and
   a2 is the argument Harry

True,
   because (eq? *a1* *a2*) is just another way to
   ask, "Are *a1* and *a2* the same atom?"

---

[1] L: eq

Is (eq? *a1* *a2*) true or false, where
   a1 is margarine, and
   a2 is butter

False,
   since the arguments *a1* and *a2* are different atoms.

How many arguments does eq? take, and
what are they?

It takes two arguments. Both of them must
be atoms.

Is (eq? *l1* *l2*) true or false, where
   l1 is ( ) and
   l2 is (strawberry)

No answer,[1]
   although ( ) is an atom, (strawberry) is a
   non-null list.

---

[1] Lists may be arguments of eq? Two lists are eq? if
they are the same list. Two lists that print the same are
equal?, but they are not necessarily eq? The beginner
should follow The Law of Eq?

The Law of Eq?

**Eq? takes two arguments. Each
must be an atom.**

Is (eq? (car *l*) *a*) true or false, where
   l is (Mary had a little lamb chop), and
   a is Mary

True,
   because (car *l*) is the atom Mary, and the
   argument *a* is also the atom Mary.

Is (eq? (cdr l) a) true or false, where
    l is (soured milk), and
    a is milk
	No answer.
	    See The Laws of Cdr and Eq?

Is (eq? (car l) (car (cdr l))) true or false,
where
    l is (beans beans we need jelly beans)
	True,
	    as this compares the first and second
	    atoms in the list.

$\Rightarrow$ **Now go make yourself a peanut butter and jelly sandwich.** $\Leftarrow$

This space reserved for

JELLY STAINS!

Exercises

1.1 Think of ten different atoms and write them down.

1.2 Using the atoms of Exercise 1.1, make up twenty different lists.

1.3 The list (all these problems) can be constructed by (cons a (cons b (cons c d))), where
$$a \text{ is all,}$$
$$b \text{ is these,}$$
$$c \text{ is problems, and}$$
$$d \text{ is ( ).}$$

Write down how you would construct the following lists:
$$\text{(all (these problems))}$$
$$\text{(all (these) problems)}$$
$$\text{((all these) problems)}$$
$$\text{((all these problems))}$$

1.4 What is (car (cons a l)), where a is french, and l is (fries);
and what is (cdr (cons a l)), where a is oranges, and l is (apples and peaches)?

1.5 Find an atom x that makes (eq? x y) true, where y is lisp. Are there any others?

1.6 If a is atom, is there a list l that makes (null? (cons a l)) true?

1.7 Determine the value of
$$\text{(cons } s \text{ } l\text{), where } s \text{ is x, and } l \text{ is y}$$
$$\text{(cons } s \text{ } l\text{), where } s \text{ is ( ), and } l \text{ is ( )}$$
$$\text{(car } s\text{), where } s \text{ is ( )}$$
$$\text{(cdr } l\text{), where } l \text{ is (( ))}$$

1.8 True or false,

(atom? (car *l*)), where *l* is ((meatballs) and spaghetti)

(null? (cdr *l*)), where *l* is ((meatballs))

(eq? (car *l*) (car (cdr *l*))), where *l* is (two meatballs)

(atom? (cons *a* *l*)), where *l* is (ball) and *a* is meat

1.9 What is

(car (cdr (cdr (car *l*)))) where *l* is ((kiwis mangoes lemons) and (more))

(car (cdr (car (cdr *l*)))) where *l* is (( ) (eggs and (bacon)) (for) (breakfast))

(car (cdr (cdr (cdr *l*)))) where *l* is (( ) ( ) ( ) (and (coffee)) please)

1.10 To get the atom and in (peanut butter and jelly on toast) we can write (car (cdr (cdr *l*))). What would you write to get:

Harry in *l*, where *l* is (apples in (Harry has a backyard))

where *l* is (apples and Harry)

where *l* is (((apples) and ((Harry))) in his backyard)

Chapter 2

Do It, Do It Again, and Again, and Again . . .

| True or false: (lat? *l*), where | True, |
| *l* is (Jack Sprat could eat no chicken fat) | because each S-expression in *l* is an atom. |

| True or false: (lat? *l*), where | False, |
| *l* is ((Jack) Sprat could eat no chicken fat) | since (car *l*) is a list. |

| True or false: (lat? *l*), where | False, |
| *l* is (Jack (Sprat could) eat no chicken fat) | since one of the S-expressions in *l* is a list. |

| True or false: (lat? *l*), where | True, |
| *l* is ( ) | because ( ) *contains* no lists, and because it does not contain any lists, it is a *lat*. |

| True or false: a lat is a list of atoms. | Every lat is a list of atoms! |

| Write the *function* lat? using some, but not necessarily all, of the following functions: car, cdr, cons, null?, atom?, and eq? | We did not expect you to know this, because you are still missing some ingredients. Go on to the next question. Good luck. |

```
(define¹ lat?
  (lambda (l)
    (cond
      ((null? l) t)
      ((atom? (car l)) (lat? (cdr l)))
      (t² nil))))
```

What is the *value* of (lat? *l*), where
  l is the argument (bacon and eggs)

t.[1]

The *application* (lat? *l*), where *l* is
    (bacon and eggs)
has the value *t*—true—because *l* is a lat.

How do you determine the answer *t* for the application
   (lat? *l*)
	We did not expect you to know this one either. The answer is determined by answering the questions asked by lat?
	   Hint: Write down the function lat? and refer to it for the next group of questions.

What is the first question asked by (lat? *l*)	(null? *l*) Note: (**cond** ...) is the one that asks questions; (**lambda** ...) creates a function; and (**define** ...) gives it a name.

What is the meaning of the *cond-line*
   ((null? *l*) t),
where
   l is (bacon and eggs)
	(null? *l*) asks if the argument *l* is the null list. If it is, then the value of the application is true. If it is not, then we ask the next question. In this case, *l* is not the null list, so we ask the next question.

What is the next question?	(atom? (car *l*)).

What is the meaning of the line
   ((atom? (car *l*)) (lat? (cdr *l*))),
where
   l is (bacon and eggs)
	(atom? (car *l*)) asks if the first S-expression of the list *l* is an atom. If (car *l*) is an atom, then we want to know if the rest of *l* is also composed only of atoms. If (car *l*) is not an atom, then we ask the next question. In this case, (car *l*) is an atom, so the value of the function is the value of (lat? (cdr *l*)).

What is the meaning of (lat? (cdr *l*))	(lat? (cdr *l*)) finds out if the rest of the list *l* is composed only of atoms, by referring to the function, but now with a new argument.
Now, what is the argument *l* for lat?	Now the argument *l* is (cdr *l*), which is (and eggs).

What is the next question?	(null? l).

What is the meaning of the line
   ((null? l) t)
where
   l is now (and eggs)
	(null? l) asks if the argument l is the null list. If it is, then the value of the application is t. If it is not, then we ask the next question. In this case, l is not the null list, so we ask the next question.

What is the next question?	(atom? (car l)).

What is the meaning of the line
   ((atom? (car l)) (lat? (cdr l)))
where
   l is (and eggs)
	(atom? (car l)) asks if (car l) is an atom. If it is an atom, then the value of the application is (lat? (cdr l)). If not, then we ask the next question. In this case, (car l) is an atom, so we want to find out if the rest of the list l is composed only of atoms.

What is the meaning of (lat? (cdr l))	(lat? (cdr l)) finds out if the rest of l is composed only of atoms, by referring again to the function lat?, but this time, with the argument (cdr l), which is (eggs).

What is the next question?	(null? l).

What is the meaning of the line
   ((null? l) t)
where
   l is now (eggs)
	(null? l) asks if the argument l is the null list. If it is, the value of the application is t, namely true. If it is not, then move to the next question. In this case, l is not null, so we ask the next question.

What is the next question?	(atom? (car l)).

What is the meaning of the line 　　((atom? (car *l*)) (lat? (cdr *l*))) where 　　*l* is now (**eggs**)	(atom? (car *l*)) asks if (car *l*) is an atom. If it is, then the value of the application is (lat? (cdr *l*)). If (car *l*) is not an atom, then ask the next question. In this case, (car *l*) is an atom, so once again we look at (lat? (cdr *l*)).
What is the meaning of (lat? (cdr *l*))	(lat? (cdr *l*)) finds out if the rest of the list *l* is composed only of atoms, by referring to the function lat?, with *l* becoming the value of (cdr *l*).
Now, what is the argument for lat?	( ).
What is the meaning of the line 　　((null? *l*) t) where 　　*l* is now ( )	(null? *l*) asks if the argument *l* is the null list. If it is, then the value of the application is the value of t. If not, then we ask the next question. In this case, ( ) is the null list. Therefore, the value of the application (lat? *l*), where *l* is (**bacon and eggs**), is *t*—true.
Do you remember the question about 　　(lat? *l*)	Probably not. The application (lat? *l*) has a value *t* if the list *l* is a list of atoms, where *l* is (**bacon and eggs**).
Can you describe what the function lat? does in your own words?	Here are our words: 　"lat? looks at each S-expression, in turn, 　and asks if each S-expression is an atom, 　until it runs out of S-expressions. If it 　runs out without encountering a list, the 　value is *t*. If it finds a list, the value is 　*nil*—false." To see how we could arrive at a value of "false," consider the next few questions.

This is the function lat?, again:

```
(define lat?
  (lambda (l)
    (cond
      ((null? l) t)
      ((atom? (car l)) (lat? (cdr l)))
      (t nil))))
```

What is the value of (lat? *l*), where
  l is now (bacon (and eggs))

nil,[1]
  since the list *l* contains an S-expression
  that is a list.

---

[1] L: To see what false is, try (eq 'a 'b).
  S: #f, but (eq? #f 'nil) is false. To see what false
is, try (eq? 'a 'b).

What is the first question?

(null? *l*).

What is the meaning of the line
  ((null? *l*) t)
where
  l is (bacon (and eggs))

(null? *l*) asks if *l* is the null list. If it is, the
value is *t*. If *l* is not null, then move to the
next question. In this case, it is not null, so
we ask the next question.

What is the next question?

(atom? (car *l*)).

What is the meaning of the line
  ((atom? (car *l*)) (lat? (cdr *l*)))
where
  l is (bacon (and eggs))

(atom? (car *l*)) asks if (car *l*) is an atom.
If it is, the value is (lat? (cdr *l*)). If it is
not, we ask the next question. In this case,
(car *l*) is an atom, so we want to check if the
rest of the list *l* is composed only of atoms.

What is the meaning of
  (lat? (cdr *l*))

(lat? (cdr *l*)) checks to see if the rest of the
list *l* is composed only of atoms, by referring
to lat? with *l* replaced by (cdr *l*).

What is the meaning of the line
  ((null? *l*) t)
where
  l is now ((and eggs))

(null? *l*) asks if *l* is the null list. If it is null,
the value is *t*. If it is not null, we ask the
next question. In this case, *l* is not null, so
move to the next question.

What is the next question?	(atom? (car *l*)).

What is the meaning of the line
  ((atom? (car *l*)) (lat? (cdr *l*)))
where
  l is now ((and **eggs**))
	(atom? (car *l*)) asks if (car *l*) is an atom. If it is, then the value is (lat? (cdr *l*)). If it is not, then we move to the next question. In this case, (car *l*) is not an atom, so we ask the next question.

What is the next question?	t.
What is the meaning of the question t?	t asks if t is true.
Is t true?	Yes, because the question t is *always* true!
t	*t.*
Why is t the last question?	Because we do not need to ask any more questions.
Why do we not need to ask any more questions?	Because a list can only be empty, or have an atom or a list in the first position.
What is the meaning of the line (t nil)	t asks if t is true. If t is true—*as it always is*—then the answer is *nil*—false.
What is)))	These are the closing or matching parentheses of (**cond**, (**lambda**, and (**define**, which appear at the beginning of a function definition. We sometimes call these "aggravation parentheses," and they are *always* put at the end.

Can you describe how we determined the value *nil* for
  (lat? *l*)
where
  l is (bacon (and eggs))
	Here is one way to say it:
	"(lat? *l*) looks at each item in its argument, to see if it is an atom. If it runs out of items before it finds a list, the value of (lat? *l*) is *t*. If it finds a list, as it did in the example (bacon (and eggs)), the value of (lat? *l*) is *nil*."

Is (**or** (null? *l*) (atom? *s*)) true or false, where
  l is ( ), and
  s is (d e f g)
	True,
	  because (null? *l*) is true where *l* is ( ).

Is (**or** (null? *l1*) (null? *l2*)) true or false, where
  l1 is (a b c), and
  l2 is ( )
	True,
	  because (null? *l2*) is true where *l2* is ( ).

Is (**or** (null? *l*) (null? *s*)) true or false, where
  l is (a b c), and
  s is (atom)
	False,
	  because neither (null? *l*) is true where *l* is (a b c) nor (null? *s*) is true where *s* is (atom).

What does (**or** ...) do?	(**or** ...) asks two questions, one at a time. If the first one is true it stops and answers true. Otherwise (**or** ...) asks the second question and answers with whatever the second question answers.

Is it true or false that *a* is a *member* of *lat*, where
  a is tea, and
  lat is (coffee tea or milk)
	True,
	  because one of the atoms of the lat,
	    (coffee tea or milk)
	  is the same as the atom *a*, namely tea.

Is (member? *a lat*) true or false, where	False,
a is poached, and	since *a* is not one of the atoms of *lat*.
lat is (fried eggs and scrambled eggs)	

This is the function member?

```
(define member?
  (lambda (a lat)
    (cond
      ((null? lat) nil)
      (t (or
           (eq? (car lat) a)
           (member? a (cdr lat)))))))
```

What is the value of (member? *a lat*), where
    a is meat, and
    lat is (mashed potatoes and meat gravy)

t,
    because the atom **meat** is one of the atoms
    of the lat,
      (mashed potatoes and meat gravy).

How do we determine the value *t* for the above application?

The value is determined by asking the questions about (member? *a lat*).
    Hint: Write down the function member? and refer to it while you work on the next group of questions.

What is the first question asked by
    (member? *a lat*)

(null? *lat*).
    This is also the first question asked by lat?

The First Commandment

Always ask null? as the first question in expressing any function.

What is the meaning of the line ((null? *lat*) nil) where *lat* is (mashed potatoes and meat gravy)	(null? *lat*) asks if *lat* is the null list. If it is, then the value is *nil*, since the atom **meat** was not found in *lat*. If not, then we ask the next question. In this case, it is not null, so we ask the next question.
What is the next question?	t.
Why is t the next question?	Because we do not need to ask any more questions.
Is t *really* a question?	Yes, t is a question whose value is always true.

What is the meaning of the line
 (t (**or**
      (eq? (car *lat*) *a*)
      (member? *a* (cdr *lat*))))
	Now that we know that *lat* is not null?, we have to find out whether the car of *lat* is the same atom as *a*, or whether *a* is somewhere in the rest of the *lat*. The question
	    (**or**
	      (eq? (car *lat*) *a*)
	      (member? *a* (cdr *lat*)))
	 does this.

Is
   (**or**
      (eq? (car *lat*) *a*)
      (member? *a* (cdr *lat*)))
 true or false, where
   a is meat, and
   lat is (mashed potatoes and meat gravy)
	We will find out by looking at each question in turn.

Is (eq? (car *lat*) *a*) true or false, where
   a is meat, and
   lat is (mashed potatoes and meat gravy)
	False,
	   because **meat** is not eq? to **mashed**,
	   the car of
	      (mashed potatoes and meat gravy).

Do It, Do It Again, and Again, and Again . . .

What is the second question for (**or** ...)	(member? *a* (cdr *lat*)). This refers to the function with the argument *lat* replaced by (cdr *lat*).
Now what are the arguments for member?	*a* is meat, and *lat* is now (cdr *lat*), specifically (potatoes and meat gravy).
What is the next question?	(null? *lat*). Remember The First Commandment.
Is (null? *lat*) true or false, where *lat* is (potatoes and meat gravy)	*nil*, namely false.
What do we do now?	Ask the next question.
What is the next question?	t.
What is t?	*t*, namely true.

What is the meaning of
  (**or**
    (eq? (car *lat*) *a*)
    (member? *a* (cdr *lat*)))
	(**or** (eq? (car *lat*) *a*) (member? *a* (cdr *lat*)))
	finds out if *a* is eq? to the car of *lat* or if *a* is a member of the cdr of *lat* by referring to the function.

Is *a* eq? to the car of *lat*	No, because *a* is meat and the car of *lat* is potatoes.
So what do we do next?	We ask (member? *a* (cdr *lat*)).

Now, what are the arguments of member?	*a* is meat, and *lat* is (and meat gravy).
What is the next question?	(null? *lat*).
What do we do now?	Ask the next question, since (null? *lat*) is false.
What is the next question?	t.

What is the value of
  (**or**
    (eq? (car *lat*) *a*)
    (member? *a* (cdr *lat*))))
	The value of (member? *a* (cdr *lat*)).

Why?	Because (eq? (car *lat*) *a*) is false.
What do we do now?	*Recur*—refer to the function with new arguments.
What are the new arguments?	*a* is meat, and *lat* is (meat gravy).
What is the next question?	(null? *lat*).
What do we do now?	Since (null? *lat*) is false, ask the next question.
What is the next question?	t.

What is the value of
(**or**
   (eq? (car *lat*) *a*)
   (member? *a* (cdr *lat*))))
	t,
	because (car *lat*), which is meat, and *a*,
	which is meat, are the same atom. There-
	fore, (**or** ...) answers with *t*.

What is the value of the application
   (member? *a* *lat*)
where
   a is meat, and
   lat is (meat gravy)
	t,
	because we have found that meat is a
	member of
	   (meat gravy).

What is the value of the application
   (member? *a* *lat*)
where
   a is meat, and
   lat is (and meat gravy)
	t,
	because meat is also a member of the *lat*
	   (and meat gravy).

What is the value of the application
   (member? *a* *lat*)
where
   a is meat, and
   lat is (potatoes and meat gravy)
	t,
	because meat is also a member of the *lat*
	   (potatoes and meat gravy).

What is the value of the application
   (member? *a* *lat*)
where
   a is meat, and
   lat is (mashed potatoes and meat gravy)
	t,
	because meat is also a member of the *lat*
	   (mashed potatoes and meat gravy).
	Of course, you noticed that this is our
	original *lat*.

Just to make sure you have it right, let's quickly run through it again:

```
(define member?
  (lambda (a lat)
    (cond
      ((null? lat) nil)
      (t (or
           (eq? (car lat) a)
           (member? a (cdr lat)))))))
```

What is the value of (member? *a lat*)
where
  a is meat, and
  lat is (mashed potatoes and meat gravy)

t.

Hint: Write down the function member? and its arguments and refer to them as you go through the next group of questions.

(null? *lat*)	No. Move to the next line.
t	Yes.
(or · (eq? (car *lat*) *a*) (member? *a* (cdr *lat*)))	Perhaps.
(eq? (car *lat*) *a*)	No. Ask the next question.
What next?	Recur with *a* and (cdr *lat*), where *a* is meat and (cdr *lat*) is (potatoes and meat gravy).
(null? *lat*)	No. Move to the next line.

t	Yes, but (eq? (car *lat*) *a*) is false. Recur with *a* and (cdr *lat*), where *a* is meat, and (cdr *lat*) is (and meat gravy).

(null? *lat*)	No. Move to the next line.

t	Yes, but (eq? (car *lat*) *a*) is false. Recur with *a* and (cdr *lat*), where *a* is meat, and (cdr *lat*) is (meat gravy).

(null? *lat*)	No. Move to the next line.

(eq? (car *lat*) *a*)	Yes, the value is *t*.

(**or**
  (eq? (car *lat*) *a*)
  (member? *a* (cdr *lat*)))
	t.

What is the value of (member? *a lat*), where
  a is meat, and
  lat is (meat gravy)
	t.

What is the value of (member? *a lat*), where
  a is meat, and
  lat is (and meat gravy)
	t.

What is the value of (member? *a lat*), where
  a is meat, and
  lat is (potatoes and meat gravy)
	t.

What is the value of (member? *a lat*), where
   a is meat, and
   lat is (mashed potatoes and meat gravy)
	t.

What is the value of (member? *a lat*), where
   a is liver, and
   lat is (bagels and lox)
	nil.

Let's work out why it is *nil*. What's the first question member? asks?	(null? *lat*).

(null? *lat*)	No. Move to the next line.

t	Yes, but (eq? (car *lat*) *a*) is false.
	   Recur with *a* and (cdr *lat*), where
	      a is liver, and
	      (cdr *lat*) is (and lox).

(null? *lat*)	No. Move to the next line.

t	Yes, but (eq? (car *lat*) *a*) is false.
	   Recur with *a* and (cdr *lat*), where
	      a is liver, and
	      (cdr *lat*) is (lox).

(null? *lat*)	No. Move to the next line.

t	Yes, but (eq? (car *lat*) *a*) is still false.
	   Recur with *a* and (cdr *lat*), where
	      a is liver, and
	      (cdr *lat*) is ( ).

(null? *lat*)	Yes.

What is the value of (member? *a lat*), where
    a is liver, and
    lat is ( )
	nil.

What is the value of
  (**or**
    (eq? (car *lat*) *a*)
    (member? *a* (cdr *lat*)))
where
  a is liver, and
  lat is (lox)
	nil.

What is the value of (member? *a lat*), where
    a is liver, and
    lat is (lox)
	nil.

What is the value of
  (**or**
    (eq? (car *lat*) *a*)
    (member? *a* (cdr *lat*)))
where
  a is liver, and
  lat is (and lox)
	nil.

What is the value of (member? *a lat*), where
    a is liver, and
    lat is (and lox)
	nil.

What is the value of
  (**or**
    (eq? (car *lat*) *a*)
    (member? *a* (cdr *lat*)))
where
  a is liver, and
  lat is (bagels and lox)
	nil.

What is the value of (member? *a lat*), where
  a is liver, and
  lat is (bagels and lox)
	nil.

Do you believe all this? Then you may rest!

This space for doodling

Exercises

For these exercises,

l1 is (german chocolate cake)
l2 is (poppy seed cake)
l3 is ((linzer) (torte) ( ))
l4 is ((bleu cheese) (and) (red) (wine))
l5 is (( ) ( ))
a1 is coffee
a2 is seed
a3 is poppy

2.1 What are the values of: (lat? *l1*), (lat? *l2*), and (lat? *l3*)?

2.2 For each case in Exercise 2.1 step through the application as we did in this chapter.

2.3 What is the value of (member? *a1 l1*), and (member? *a2 l2*)?
Step through the application for each case.

2.4 Most Lisp dialects have an (**if** ...)-form. In general an (**if** ...)-form looks like this:

$$(\textbf{if } aexp\ bexp\ cexp).$$

When *aexp* is true, (**if** *aexp bexp cexp*) is *bexp*; when it is false, (**if** *aexp bexp cexp*) is *cexp*. For example,

```
(cond
   ((null? l) nil)
   (t (or
        (eq? (car l) a)
        (member? a (cdr l)))))
```

in member? can be replaced by:

```
(if (null? l)
   nil
   (or
      (eq? (car l) a)
      (member? a (cdr l))))
```

Rewrite all the functions in the chapter using (**if** ...) instead of (**cond** ...).

2.5 Write the function nonlat? which determines whether a list is the empty list or does not contain atomic S-expressions.

Example: (nonlat? *l1*) is false,
    (nonlat? *l2*) is false,
    (nonlat? *l3*) is false,
    (nonlat? *l4*) is true.

2.6 Write a function member-cake? which determines whether a lat contains the atom cake.

Example: (member-cake? *l1*) is true,
    (member-cake? *l2*) is true,
    (member-cake? *l5*) is false.

2.7 Consider the following new definition of member?

```
(define member2?
  (lambda (a lat)
    (cond
      ((null? lat) nil)
      (t (or
           (member2? a (cdr lat))
           (eq? a (car lat)))))))
```

Do (member2? *a l*) and (member? *a l*) give the same answer when we use the same arguments? Consider the examples *a1* and *l1*, *a1* and *l2*, and *a2* and *l2*.

2.8 Step through the applications (member? *a3 l2*) and (member2? *a3 l2*). Compare the steps of the two applications.

2.9 What happens when you step through (member? *a2 l3*)? Fix this problem by having member? ignore lists.

2.10 The function member? tells whether some atom appears *at least once* in a lat. Write a function member-twice? which tells whether some atom appears *at least twice* in a lat.

Chapter 3

Cons The Magnificent

What is (rember *a lat*), where
    a is mint, and
    lat is (lamb chops and mint jelly)
	(lamb chops and jelly)
	    "Rember" stands for *rem*ove a mem*ber*.

(rember *a lat*), where
    a is mint, and
    lat is (lamb chops and
        mint flavored mint jelly)
	(lamb chops and flavored mint jelly).

(rember *a lat*), where
    a is toast, and
    lat is (bacon lettuce and tomato)
	(bacon lettuce and tomato).

(rember *a lat*), where
    a is cup, and
    lat is (coffee cup tea cup and hick cup)
	(coffee tea cup and hick cup).

What does (rember *a lat*) do?	It takes an atom and a lat as its arguments, and makes a new lat with the first occurrence of the atom in the old lat removed.
What steps will we use to do this?	First we will test (null? *lat*) —The First Commandment.
And if (null? *lat*) is true?	Return ( ).
What do we know if (null? *lat*) is not true?	We know that there must be at least one atom in the lat.
Is there any other question we should ask about the lat?	No. Either a lat is empty or it contains at least one atom.

What do we do if we know that the lat contains at least one atom?	We will ask whether *a* is equal to (car *lat*).

How do we ask questions?	By using
	(**cond**
	   (_____ _____)
	   (_____ _____)).

How do we ask if *a* is the same as (car *lat*)	(eq? (car *lat*) *a*).
What would be the value of (rember *a lat*) if *a* were the same as (car *lat*)	(cdr *lat*).
What do we do if *a* is not the same as (car *lat*)	We will want to keep (car *lat*), but also find out if *a* is somewhere in the rest of the lat.
How do we replace the first occurrence of *a* in the rest of *lat*	(rember *a* (cdr *lat*)).
Is there any other question we should ask?	No.

Now, let's write down what we have so far:

```
(define rember
  (lambda (a lat)
    (cond
      ((null? lat) (quote ( )))
      (t (cond
           ((eq? (car lat) a) (cdr lat))
           (t (rember a (cdr lat)))))))))
```

What is the value of (rember *a lat*) where
   a is bacon, and
   lat is (bacon lettuce and tomato)

(lettuce and tomato).
   Hint: Write down the function rember and its arguments, and refer to them as you go through the next sequence of questions.

Now, let's see if this function works. What is the first question?	(null? *lat*).
What do we do now?	Move to the next line and ask the next question.
t	*t*.
What next?	Ask the next question.
(eq? (car *lat*) *a*)	Yes, so the value is (cdr *lat*). In this case, it is the list (lettuce and tomato).
Is this the correct value?	Yes, because the above list is the original list without the atom **bacon**.
But did we *really* use a good example?	Who knows? But the proof of the pudding is in the eating, so let's try another example.
What does rember do?	It takes an atom and a lat as its arguments, and makes a new lat with the first occurrence of the atom in the old lat removed.
What will we do?	We will compare each atom of the lat with the atom *a*, and if the comparison fails we will build a list which begins with the atom we just compared.

What is the value of (rember *a* *lat*), where
  a is **and**, and
  lat is (bacon lettuce and tomato)
	(bacon lettuce tomato).

Let us see if our function rember works. What is the first question asked by rember	(null? *lat*).
What do we do now?	Move to the next line, and ask the next question.
t	*t*, so ask the next question.
(eq? (car *lat*) *a*)	No, so move to the next line.
What is the meaning of (t (rember *a* (cdr *lat*)))	t asks if t is true—as it always is—and the rest of the line says to recur with *a* and (cdr *lat*), where *a* is **and**, and (cdr *lat*) is (lettuce and tomato).
(null? *lat*)	No, so move to the next line.
t	*t*.
(eq? (car *lat*) *a*)	No, so move to the next line.
What is the meaning of (t (rember *a* (cdr *lat*)))	Recur, where *a* is **and**, and (cdr *lat*) is (and tomato).
(null? *lat*)	No, so move to the next line, and ask the next question.
t	*t*.

(eq? (car *lat*) *a*)	Yes.
What is the value of the application (rember *a* *lat*)	(cdr *lat*), that is, (tomato).
Is this correct?	No, since (tomato) is not the list (bacon lettuce and tomato) with only *a*, namely and, removed.
What did we do wrong?	We dropped and, but we also lost all the atoms preceding and.
How can we keep from losing the atoms bacon and lettuce	We use *Cons The Magnificent*. Remember cons, from Chapter 1?

The Second Commandment

Use cons to build lists.

Let's see what happens when we use *cons*:

```
(define rember
  (lambda (a lat)
    (cond
      ((null? lat) (quote ( )))
      (t (cond
           ((eq? (car lat) a) (cdr lat))
           (t (cons (car lat)
                (rember
                  a (cdr lat)))))))))
```

What is the value of (rember *a* *lat*), where
  a is and, and
  lat is (bacon lettuce and tomato)

(bacon lettuce tomato).

Make a copy of this function with cons and the arguments *a* and *lat* so you can refer to it for the following questions.

What is the first question?	(null? *lat*).
What do we do now?	Ask the next question.
t	Yes, of course.
(eq? (car *lat*) *a*)	No, so move to the next line.

What is the meaning of
  (cons
    (car *lat*)
    (rember *a* (cdr *lat*)))
where
  a is and, and
  lat is (bacon lettuce and tomato)
	cons (car *lat*)—that is, bacon—onto the value of
	  (rember *a* (cdr *lat*)).
	But since we don't know the value of (rember *a* (cdr *lat*)) yet, we will have to find it before we can cons (car *lat*) onto it.

What is the meaning of (rember *a* (cdr *lat*))	This refers to the function, with *lat* replaced by (cdr *lat*), that is, (lettuce and tomato).
(null? *lat*)	No, so move to the next line.
t	Yes, ask the next question.
(eq? (car *lat*) *a*)	No, so move to the next line.

What is the meaning of
  (cons
    (car *lat*)
    (rember *a* (cdr *lat*)))
	It means cons (car *lat*), namely lettuce, onto the value of (rember *a* (cdr *lat*)). But since we don't know the value, we must first find that value before cons*ing* (car *lat*) onto it.

What is the meaning of (rember *a* (cdr *lat*))	This refers to the function with *lat* replaced by (cdr *lat*), that is, (and tomato).
(null? *lat*)	No, so ask the next question.
t	Still.
(eq? (car *lat*) *a*)	Yes.
What is the value of the line ((eq? (car *lat*) *a*) (cdr *lat*))	(cdr *lat*), that is, (tomato).
Are we finished?	Certainly not! We know what (rember *a lat*) is when *lat* is (and tomato), but we don't yet know what it is when *lat* is (lettuce and tomato) or (bacon lettuce and tomato).

We now have a value for
(rember *a* (cdr *lat*)), where
    a is and,
and
    (cdr *lat*) is (and tomato)
This value is (tomato). What next?
	Recall that we wanted to cons lettuce onto the value of (rember *a* (cdr *lat*)), where *a* was and and (cdr *lat*) was (and tomato). Now that we have this value, which is (tomato), we can cons lettuce onto this value.

What is the result when we cons lettuce onto (tomato)	(lettuce tomato).

What does (lettuce tomato) represent?	It represents the value of
	    (cons
	        (car *lat*)
	        (rember *a* (cdr *lat*))),
	when
	    lat was (lettuce and tomato), and
	    (rember *a* (cdr *lat*)) was (tomato).

Are we finished yet?	Not quite. So far we know what
	(rember *a lat*) is when
	    lat is (lettuce and tomato),
	but we don't yet know what it is when
	    lat is (bacon lettuce and tomato).

We now have a value for (rember *a* (cdr *lat*))
when
    a is and, and
    (cdr *lat*) is (lettuce and tomato).
This value is (lettuce tomato). This is not
the final value, so what must we do again?
	Recall that, at one time, we wanted to cons
	bacon onto the value of (rember *a* (cdr *lat*)),
	when
	    a was and,
	and
	    (cdr *lat*) was (lettuce and tomato).
	Now that we have this value, which is
	    (lettuce tomato),
	we can cons bacon onto this value.

What is the result when we cons bacon onto (lettuce tomato)	(bacon lettuce tomato).

What does (bacon lettuce tomato)
represent?[†]
 	
――――――――――
† lunch?
	It represents the value of
	    (cons
	        (car *lat*)
	        (rember *a* (cdr *lat*))),
	when
	    lat was (bacon lettuce and tomato), and
	    (rember *a* (cdr *lat*)) was (lettuce tomato).

Are we finished yet?	Yes.

Can you put in your own words how we
determined the final value
    (bacon lettuce tomato)
	In our words:
	    "Rember checked each atom of the lat, one
	    at a time, to see if it was the same as the
	    atom and. If the car was not the same as
	    the atom, we saved it to be cons*ed* to the
	    final value later. When rember found the
	    atom and, it dropped it, and cons*ed* the
	    previous atoms onto the rest of the lat, in
	    reverse order."

Can you rewrite rember so that it reflects the above description?	Yes, we can simplify it.

```
(define rember
  (lambda (a lat)
    (cond
      ((null? lat) (quote ( )))
      ((eq? (car lat) a) (cdr lat))
      (t (cons (car lat)
              (rember a (cdr lat))))))))
```

Do you think this is simpler?	Functions like rember can always be simplified in this manner.

So why don't we simplify yet?	Because then a function's structure does not coincide with its data's structure.

Let's see if the new rember is the same as the old one. What is the value of the application
 	
    (rember *a lat*),
where
    a is and, and
    lat is (bacon lettuce and tomato)
	(bacon lettuce tomato).
	    Hint: Write down the function rember and its arguments and refer to them as you go through the next sequence of questions.

(null? *lat*)	No.

(eq? (car *lat*) *a*)	No.

t	Yes, so the value is
	    (cons
	        (car *lat*)
	        (rember *a* (cdr *lat*))).

What is the meaning of
  (cons
    (car *lat*)
    (rember *a* (cdr *lat*)))
	This says to refer to the function rember, but with the argument *lat* replaced by (cdr *lat*), and that *after* we arrive at a value for (rember *a* (cdr *lat*)) we will cons (car *lat*), namely bacon, onto it.

(null? *lat*)	No.
(eq? (car *lat*) *a*)	No.

t	Yes, so the value is
	  (cons
	    (car *lat*)
	    (rember *a* (cdr *lat*))).

What is the meaning of
  (cons
    (car *lat*)
    (rember *a* (cdr *lat*)))
	This says we recur using the function rember, with the argument *lat* replaced by (cdr *lat*), and that *after* we arrive at a value for (rember *a* (cdr *lat*)), we will cons (car *lat*), namely lettuce, onto it.

(null? *lat*)	No.
(eq? (car *lat*) *a*)	Yes.
What is the value of the line ((eq? (car *lat*) *a*) (cdr *lat*))	It is (cdr *lat*), that is, (tomato).
Now what?	Now cons (car *lat*), that is, lettuce, onto (tomato).

Now what?	Now cons (car *lat*), that is, bacon, onto (lettuce tomato).

Now that we have completed rember, try this example: 　(rember *a lat*), where 　*a* is sauce, and 　*lat* is (soy sauce and tomato sauce)	(rember *a lat*) is (soy and tomato sauce).

What is (firsts *l*), where 　*l* is ((apple peach pumpkin) 　　(plum pear cherry) 　　(grape raisin pea) 　　(bean carrot eggplant))	(apple plum grape bean).

What is (firsts *l*), where 　*l* is ((a b) (c d) (e f))	(a c e).

What is (firsts *l*), where 　*l* is ( )	( ).

What is (firsts *l*), where 　*l* is ((five plums) (four) 　　(eleven green oranges))	(five four eleven).

In your own words, what does (firsts *l*) do?	We tried the following: 　"Firsts takes one argument, a list, which must either be a null list, or contain only non-null lists. It builds another list composed of the first S-expression of each internal list."

See if you can write the function firsts. *Remember the Commandments!*	Believe it or not, you can probably write the following:

> (**define** firsts
>   (**lambda** (*l*)
>   (**cond**
>   ((null? *l*) _____)
>   (t (cons _____ (firsts (cdr *l*)))))))

Why (**define** firsts (**lambda** (*l*)	Because we always state the function name, (**lambda**, and the argument(s) of the function.
Why (**cond**	Because we need to ask questions about the actual arguments.
Why ((null? *l*) _____)	The First Commandment.
Why (t	Because we only have two questions to ask about the list *l*: either it is the null list, or it contains at least one non-null list.
Why (t	See above. And because the last question is always t.
Why (cons	Because we are building a list —The Second Commandment.
Why (firsts (cdr *l*))	Because we can only look at one S-expression at a time. To do this, we must recur.

Why)))	Because these are the matching parentheses for (**cond**, (**lambda**, and (**define**, and they always appear at the end of a function definition.
Keeping in mind the definition of (firsts *l*), what is a *typical element* of the value of (firsts *l*), where *l* is ((a b) (c d) (e f))	a.
What is another typical element?	c or e.
Consider the function seconds. What would be a typical element of the value of (seconds *l*), where *l* is ((a b) (c d) (e f))	b, d, or f.
How do we *describe* a typical element for (firsts *l*)	As the car of (car *l*), that is, (car (car *l*)). See Chapter 1.
When we find a typical element of (firsts *l*), what do we do with it?	We cons it onto the recursion, that is, (firsts (cdr *l*)).

The Third Commandment

When building a list, describe the first typical element, and then cons it onto the natural recursion.

With The Third Commandment, we can now fill in more of the function firsts. What does the last line look like now?

(t (cons (car (car *l*)) (firsts (cdr *l*)))).

typical natural
element recursion

What does (firsts *l*) do

```
(define firsts
  (lambda (l)
    (cond
      ((null? l) _____ )
      (t (cons (car (car l))
          (firsts (cdr l)))))))
```

where
 l is ((a b) (c d) (e f))

Nothing yet. We are still missing one important ingredient in our recipe. The first line ((null? *l*) _____) needs a value for the case where *l* *is* the null list. We can, however, proceed without it for now.

(null? *l*), where
 l is ((a b) (c d) (e f))

No, so move to the next line.

What is the meaning of
 (cons
  (car (car *l*))
  (firsts (cdr *l*)))

It saves (car (car *l*)) to cons onto (firsts (cdr *l*)). To find (firsts (cdr *l*)), we refer to the function with the new argument (cdr *l*).

(null? *l*), where
 l is ((c d) (e f))

No, so move to the next line.

What is the meaning of
 (cons
  (car (car *l*))
  (firsts (cdr *l*)))

Save (car (car *l*)), and recur with (firsts (cdr *l*)).

(null? *l*), where *l* is ((**e f**))	No, so move to the next line.

What is the meaning of
  (cons
    (car (car *l*))
    (firsts (cdr *l*)))
	Save (car (car *l*)), and recur with
	(firsts (cdr *l*)).

(null? *l*)	Yes.
Now, what is the value of the line ((null? *l*) ————)	There is no value; something is missing.
What do we need to cons atoms onto?	A list. Remember The Law of Cons?
What value can we give when (null? *l*) is true, for the purpose of cons*ing*?	Since the final value must be a list, we cannot use t or nil. Let's try (**quote** ( )).

With ( ) as a value, we now have three cons steps to go back and pick up.

    I. We need to:
        1. cons e onto ( )
        2. cons c onto the value of 1
        3. cons a onto the value of 2

or, alternatively,

    II. We need to:
        1. cons a onto the value of 2
        2. cons c onto the value of 3
        3. cons e onto ( )

or, alternatively,

    III. We need to:
        cons a onto
          the cons of c onto
            the cons of e onto
              ( )

In any case, what is the final value of (firsts *l*)

(a c e).

With which of the three alternatives do you feel most comfortable?

Correct! Now you use that one.

What is
  (insertR *new old lat*)
where
  new is topping,
  old is fudge, and
  lat is (ice cream with fudge for dessert)

(ice cream with fudge topping for dessert).

(insertR *new old lat*), where
  new is jalapeño,
  old is and, and
  lat is (tacos tamales and salsa)

(tacos tamales and jalapeño salsa).

(insertR *new old lat*), where
   new is e,
   old is d, and
   lat is (a b c d f g d h)
	(a b c d e f g d h).

In your own words, what does
   (insertR *new old lat*) do?
	In our words:
	   "It takes three arguments: the atoms *new*
	   and *old*, and a lat. InsertR builds a lat
	   with *new* inserted to the *right* of the first
	   occurrence of *old*."

See if you can write the first three lines of
the function insertR.
	(**define** insertR
	  (**lambda** (*new old lat*)
	    (**cond**

Which argument will change when we recur with insertR?	*lat*, because we can only look at one of its atoms at a time.

How many questions can we ask about *lat*?	Two.
	   A lat is either the null list or a non-null
	   list of atoms.

Which questions will we ask?	First, we will ask (null? *lat*). Second, we will ask t, because t is always the last question.
What do we know if (null? *lat*) is not true?	We know that there is at least one element in *lat*.
Which questions will we ask about the first element?	First, we will ask (eq? (car *lat*) *old*). Then we ask t, because there are no other interest- ing cases.

Now see if you can write the whole function insertR

```
(define insertR
  (lambda (new old lat)
    (cond
      ((null? lat) (quote ()))
      (t (cond
           ( _____ _____ )
           ( _____ _____ ))))))
```

Here is our first attempt.

```
(define insertR
  (lambda (new old lat)
    (cond
      ((null? lat) (quote ()))
      (t (cond
           ((eq? (car lat) old) (cdr lat))
           (t (cons (car lat)
                (insertR
                  new old (cdr lat)))))))))
```

What is the value of the insertR we just wrote, where
   new is topping,
   old is fudge, and
   lat is (ice cream with fudge for dessert)

(ice cream with for dessert).

Notice that so far, this is the same as rember; but for insertR, what do we do when (eq? (car *lat*) *old*) is true?

When (car *lat*) is the same as *old*, we want to insert *new* to the right.

How is this done?

Let's try cons*ing* *new* onto (cdr *lat*).

Now we have

```
(define insertR
  (lambda (new old lat)
    (cond
      ((null? lat) (quote ()))
      (t (cond
           ((eq? (car lat) old)
            (cons new (cdr lat)))
           (t (cons (car lat)
                (insertR
                  new old (cdr lat)))))))))
```

Yes.

So what is (insertR *new old lat*) now, where
   new is topping,
   old is fudge, and
   lat is (ice cream with fudge for dessert)

(ice cream with topping for dessert).

Is this the list we wanted?

No, we have only *replaced* fudge with topping.

What still needs to be done?

Somehow we need to include the atom which is the same as *old* before the atom *new*.

How can we include *old* before *new*?

Try cons*ing* old onto (cons *new* (cdr *lat*)).

Now you should be able to write the rest of the function insertR. Do it.

```
(define insertR
  (lambda (new old lat)
    (cond
      ((null? lat) (quote ( )))
      (t (cond
           ((eq? (car lat) old)
            (cons old
              (cons new (cdr lat))))
           (t (cons (car lat)
                (insertR
                  new old (cdr lat)))))))))
```

When *new* is topping, *old* is fudge, and *lat* is (ice cream with fudge for dessert), the value of the application, (insertR *new old lat*), is (ice cream with fudge topping for dessert).

If you got this right, have one.

Now try insertL.

Hint: insertL inserts the atom *new* to the *left* of the first occurrence of the atom *old* in *lat*.

This much is easy, right?

```
(define insertL
  (lambda (new old lat)
    (cond
      ((null? lat) (quote ( )))
      (t (cond
           ((eq? (car lat) old)
            (cons new
              (cons old (cdr lat))))
           (t (cons (car lat)
                (insertL
                  new old (cdr lat)))))))))
```

Did you think of a different way to do it?

For example,
```
      ((eq? (car lat) old)
       (cons new (cons old (cdr lat))))
```
could have been
```
      ((eq? (car lat) old)
       (cons new lat)),
```
since (cons *old* (cdr *lat*)) where *old* is eq? to (car *lat*) is the same as *lat*.

Now try subst.

Hint: (subst *new old lat*) replaces the first occurrence of *old* in the *lat* with the atom *new*. For example, where
  new is topping,
  old is fudge, and
  lat is (ice cream with fudge for dessert),
the value is
  (ice cream with topping for dessert)

Now you have the idea.

Obviously,

```
(define subst
  (lambda (new old lat)
    (cond
      ((null? lat) (quote ( )))
      (t (cond
           ((eq? (car lat) old)
            (cons new (cdr lat)))
           (t (cons (car lat)
                (subst
                  new old (cdr lat)))))))))
```

This is the same as our second attempt at insertR.

Go cons a piece of cake onto your mouth.

Now try subst2.

Hint:

(subst2 *new o1 o2 lat*)

replaces either the first occurrence of *o1*
or the first occurrence of *o2* by *new*. For
example, where

   new is vanilla,

   o1 is chocolate,

   o2 is banana, and

   lat is (banana ice cream

      with chocolate topping)

the value is

   (vanilla ice cream

   with chocolate topping).

```
(define subst2
  (lambda (new o1 o2 lat)
    (cond
      ((null? lat) (quote ( )))
      (t (cond
           ((eq? (car lat) o1)
            (cons new (cdr lat)))
           ((eq? (car lat) o2)
            (cons new (cdr lat)))
           (t (cons (car lat)
                (subst2 new
                  o1 o2 (cdr lat)))))))))
```

Did you think of a better way?

Replace the two eq? lines about the (car *lat*)
by

  ((**or** (eq? (car *lat*) *o1*) (eq? (car *lat*) *o2*))
  (cons *new* (cdr *lat*))).

If you got the last function, go and repeat the cake-consing

Draw a picture of "**Cons** The Magnificent" here.

Exercises

For these exercises,

> $l1$ is ((paella spanish) (wine red) (and beans))
> $l2$ is ( )
> $l3$ is (cincinnati chili)
> $l4$ is (texas hot chili)
> $l5$ is (soy sauce and tomato sauce)
> $l6$ is ((spanish) ( ) (paella))
> $l7$ is ((and hot) (but dogs))
> $a1$ is chili
> $a2$ is hot
> $a3$ is spicy
> $a4$ is sauce
> $a5$ is soy

3.1 Write the function seconds which takes a list of lats and makes a new lat consisting of the second atom from each lat in the list.

Example: (seconds $l1$) is (spanish red beans)
       (seconds $l2$) is ( )
       (seconds $l7$) is (hot dogs)

3.2 Write the function dupla of a and l which makes a new lat containing as many a's as there are elements in l.

Example: (dupla $a2$ $l4$) is (hot hot hot)
       (dupla $a2$ $l2$) is ( )
       (dupla $a1$ $l5$) is (chili chili chili chili chili)

3.3 Write the function double of a and l which is a converse to rember. The function doubles the first a in l instead of removing it.

Example: (double $a2$ $l2$) is ( )
       (double $a1$ $l3$) is (cincinnati chili chili)
       (double $a2$ $l4$) is (texas hot hot chili)

3.4 Write the function subst-sauce of *a* and *l* which substitutes *a* for the first atom sauce in *l*.

Example: (subst-sauce *a1 l4*) is (texas hot chili)
         (subst-sauce *a1 l5*) is (soy chili and tomato sauce)
         (subst-sauce *a4 l2*) is ( )

3.5 Write the function subst3 of *new, o1, o2, o3,* and *lat* which—like subst2—replaces the first occurrence of either *o1, o2,* or *o3* in *lat* by *new.*

Example: (subst3 *a5 a1 a2 a4 l5*) is (soy soy and tomato sauce)
         (subst3 *a4 a1 a2 a3 l4*) is (texas sauce chili)
         (subst3 *a3 a1 a2 a5 l2*) is ( )

3.6 Write the function substN of *new, slat,* and *lat* which replaces the first atom in *lat* that also occurs in *slat* by the atom *new.*

Example: (substN *a2 l3 l4*) is (texas hot hot)
         (substN *a4 l3 l5*) is (soy sauce and tomato sauce)
         (substN *a4 l3 l2*) is ( )

3.7 Step through the application (rember *a4 l5*). Also step through (insertR *a5 a2 l5*) for the "bad" definitions of insertR.

3.8 Determine the *typical elements* and the *natural recursions* of the functions that you have written so far.

3.9 Write the function rember2 of *a* and *l* which removes the second occurrence of *a* in *l*.

Example: (rember2 *a1 l3*) is (cincinnati chili)
         (rember2 *a4 l5*) is (soy sauce and tomato)
         (rember2 *a4 l2*) is ( )

Hint: Use the function rember.

3.10 Consider the functions insertR, insertL, and subst. They are all very similar. Write the functions next to each other and draw boxes around the parts that they have in common. Can you see what rember has in common with these functions?

Chapter 4

Numbers Games

Is 14 an atom?	Yes, because all *numbers* are atoms.

Is (atom? n) true or false, where n is 14	True, because 14 is an atom.

Is -3 a number?	Yes.
	   However, we do not consider negative
	   numbers in this book.

Is 3.1415 a number?	Yes.
	   However, we consider only whole numbers
	   in this book.

Are -3 and 3.1415 numbers?	Yes.
	   However, the only numbers we use are
	   the nonnegative integers (i.e., 0, 1, 2, 3,
	   4, ...).

What is (add1[1] n), where n is 67	68

---

[1]   L: 1+
    S: See Preface, page xiii.

What is (sub1[1] n), where n is 5	4

---

[1]   L: 1-
    S: See Preface, page xiii.

What is (sub1 *n*), where *n* is 0	No answer.[1]

---

[1] (sub1 *n*), where *n* is 0, has no answer because we consider only nonnegative numbers. In practice, this result is -1.

What is (zero?[1] *n*) true or false, where
    n is 0

True.

---

[1] L: **zerop**

Is (zero? *n*) true or false, where
    n is 1492

False.

What is (+ *n* *m*), where
    n is 46, and
    m is 12

58

Try to write the function +
    Hint: It uses zero?, add1, and sub1.

```
(define +
  (lambda (n m)
    (cond
      ((zero? m) n)
      (t (add1 (+ n (sub1 m)))))))
```

Wasn't that easy?

But didn't we just violate The First Commandment?

Yes! However, we can treat zero? like null? since zero? asks if a *number* is empty and null? asks if a *list* is empty.

If zero? is like null?, is add1 like cons?

Yes! cons builds lists and add1 builds numbers.

What is $(- \; n \; m)$, where
  n is 8, and
  m is 3
	5

What is $(- \; n \; m)$, where
  n is 17, and
  m is 9
	8

What is $(- \; n \; m)$, where
  n is 3, and
  m is 5
	No answer.[1]
	
	———————————
	[1] No negative numbers

Try to write the function $-$ Hint: Use sub1.	How about this:

```
(define −
  (lambda (n m)
    (cond
      ((zero? m) n)
      (t (sub1 (− n (sub1 m)))))))
```

Can you describe how $(- \; n \; m)$ does what it does?	It takes two numbers as arguments, and reduces the second until it hits zero. It subtracts one from the first number as many times as it did to cause the second one to reach zero.

Is this a *vec*? (2 11 3 79 47 6)	Yes, because it is a list of numbers.

Is this a vec? (1 2 8 x 4 3)	No, it is just a list of atoms.

Is this a vec? (3 (7 4) 13 9)	No, because it is not a list of numbers. (7 4) is not a number.
Is this a vec? ( )	Yes, it is a list of zero numbers. This special case is the *empty vec*.
What is (addvec *vec*), where *vec* is (3 5 2 8)	18
What is (addvec *vec*), where *vec* is (15 6 7 12 3)	43
What does addvec do?	It *builds a number* by totalling all the numbers in its *argument*.
What is the natural way to build *numbers* from a list, just as cons is the natural way to build *lists*?	By using + in place of cons.
When building lists with cons, the value of the terminal condition is ( ). What should be the value of the terminal condition when building numbers with +	0
What is the natural terminal condition for a list?	(null? *l*).
What is the natural terminal condition for a vec?	(null? *vec*).

When you want to build a number from a list of numbers, what should the terminal condition line look like?	((null? *vec*) 0), just as ((null? *l*) (**quote** ( ))) is often the terminal condition line for lists.
What is the terminal condition line of addvec	((null? *vec*) 0).
How is a lat defined?	It is either an empty lat, or it contains an atom and a rest, where rest is again a lat.
How is a vec defined?	It is either an empty vec, or it contains a number and a rest, where rest is again a vec.
What is used in the natural recursion on a list?	(cdr *lat*).
What is used in the natural recursion on a vec?	(cdr *vec*).
Why?	Because the rest of a non-empty list is a list and the rest of a non-empty vec is a vec.
How many questions do we need to ask about a list?	Two.
How many questions do we need to ask about a vec?	Two, because it is either empty or it is a number and a rest, which is again a vec.
How is a number defined?	It is either zero or it is one added to a rest, where rest is again a number.

What is the natural terminal condition for numbers?	(zero? n).
What is the natural recursion on a number?	(sub1 n).
How many questions do we need to ask about a number?	Two.

The Fourth Commandment

(*preliminary*)

When recurring on a list of atoms, *lat*, or a vec, *vec*, ask two questions about them, and use (cdr *lat*) **or** (cdr *vec*) **for the natural recursion.**

When recurring on a number, n, ask two questions, and use (sub1 n) **for the natural recursion.**

What does cons do?	It builds lists.
What does addvec do?	It builds a number by totalling all the numbers in a vec.
What is the terminal condition line of addvec	((null? *vec*) 0).
What is the natural recursion for addvec	(addvec (cdr *vec*)).
What does addvec use to build a number?	It uses + because + *builds numbers!*

What will be the last line in the function:

(**define** addvec
(**lambda** (*vec*)
(**cond**
((null? *vec*) 0)
(t _____))))

(t (+ (car *vec*) (addvec (cdr *vec*)))).
Notice the similarity between this line,
and the last line of the function rember:
  (t (cons (car *lat*) (rember *a* (cdr *lat*))))).

What is (× *n* *m*), where
  n is 5, and
  m is 3

15

What is (× *n* *m*), where
  n is 13, and
  m is 4

52

What does (× *n* *m*) do?

It builds up a number by adding *n* up *m* times.

What is the terminal condition line for ×

((zero? *m*) 0), because $n \times 0 = 0$.

Since (zero? *m*) is the terminal condition, *m* must eventually be reduced to zero. What function is used to do this?

sub1.

What is another name for (× *n* (sub1 *m*)) in this case?

Natural recursion.

Try to write the function ×.

(**define** ×
(**lambda** (*n* *m*)
(**cond**
((zero? *m*) 0)
(t (+ *n* (× *n* (sub1 *m*)))))))))

What is (× *n* *m*), where
  n is 12, and
  m is 3
	36,
	  but let's follow through the function one
	  time to see how we get this value.

(zero? *m*)	No.
What is the meaning of (+ *n* (× *n* (sub1 *m*)))	It adds *n*, that is 12, to the natural recursion. If × is correct then (× 12 (sub1 3)) should be 24.
What are the new arguments of (× *n* *m*)	*n* is 12, and *m* is 2.
(zero? *m*)	No.
What is the meaning of (+ *n* (× *n* (sub1 *m*)))	It adds *n*, that is 12, to (× *n* (sub1 *m*)).
What are the new arguments of (× *n* *m*)	*n* is 12, and *m* is 1.
(zero? *m*)	No.
What is the meaning of (+ *n* (× *n* (sub1 *m*)))	It adds *n*, that is 12, to (× *n* (sub1 *m*)).
What is the value of the line ((zero? *m*) 0)	0, because (zero? *m*) is now true.
Are we finished yet?	No.

Why not?	Because we still have three $+es$ to pick up.

What is the value of the application?	$+$ 12 to $+$ 12 to $+$ 12 to 0 yielding 36. Notice that n has been $+ed$ m times.

Argue, using equations, that $\times$ is the conventional multiplication of nonnegative integers, where n is 12 and m is 3.	$12 \times 3 = 12 \times 2 + 12$

$$12 \times 3 = 12 \times 2 + 12$$
$$12 \times 2 = 12 \times 1 + 12$$
$$12 \times 1 = 12 \times 0 + 12$$
$$12 \times 0 = 0$$
$$12 \times 3 = 0 + 12 + 12 + 12$$
$$= 36$$

Which is as we expected. This technique works for all recursive functions, not just those that use numbers. You can use this approach to write functions as well as to argue their correctness.

Again, why is 0 the value for the terminal condition line in $\times$	Because 0 will not affect $+$. That is, $n + 0 = n$.

The Fifth Commandment

When building a value with $+$, always use 0 for the value of the terminating line, for adding 0 does not change the value of an addition.

When building a value with $\times$, always use 1 for the value of the terminating line, for multiplying by 1 does not change the value of a multiplication.

When building a value with cons, always consider ( ) for the value of the terminating line.

What is (vec+ *vec1* *vec2*), where
    vec1 is (3 6 9 11 4), and
    vec2 is (8 5 2 0 7)
	(11 11 11 11 11).

What is (vec+ *vec1* *vec2*), where
    vec1 is (2 3), and
    vec2 is (4 6)
	(6 9).

What does (vec+ *vec1* *vec2*) do?	It adds the first number of *vec1* to the first number of *vec2*, then it adds the second number of *vec1* to the second number of *vec2*, and so on, building a vec of the answers, for vecs of the same length.
What is unusual about vec+	It looks at each element of two vecs at the same time, or in other words, it recurs on two vecs.
If you recur on one vec how many questions do you have to ask?	Two, they are (null? *vec*) and t.
When recurring on two vecs, how many questions need to be asked about the vecs?	Four: if the first vec is empty or non-empty, and if the second vec is empty or non-empty.
Can the first *vec* be ( ) at the same time as the second is other than ( )	No, because the vecs are of the same length.
How many questions do we really need?	Two.

Write the function vec+.	```
	(define vec+
	  (lambda (vec1 vec2)
	    (cond
	      ((null? vec1) (quote ( )))
	      (t (cons (+ (car vec1) (car vec2))
	           (vec+
	             (cdr vec1) (cdr vec2))))))))
	``

What are the arguments of + in the last line?	(car *vec1*) and (car *vec2*).

What are the arguments of cons in the last line?	(+ (car *vec1*) (car *vec2*)), and (vec+ (cdr *vec1*) (cdr *vec2*)).

What is (vec+ *vec1* *vec2*), where
  vec1 is (3 7), and
  vec2 is (4 6)
	(7 13).
	  But let's see how it works.

(null? *vec1*)	No.

(cons
  (+ (car *vec1*) (car *vec2*))
  (vec+ (cdr *vec1*) (cdr *vec2*)))
	cons 7 onto the natural recursion:
	  (vec+ (cdr *vec1*) (cdr *vec2*)).

Why does the natural recursion include the cdr of both arguments?	Because the typical element of the final value uses the car of *both* vecs, so now we are ready to consider the rest of *both* vecs.

(null? *vec1*), where
  vec1 is now (7), and
  vec2 is now (6)
	No.

(cons
  (+ (car *vec1*) (car *vec2*))
  (vec+ (cdr *vec1*) (cdr *vec2*)))
	cons 13 onto the natural recursion.

(null? *vec1*)	Yes.
What is the value of the line ((null? *vec1*) (**quote** ( )))	( ).
What is the value of the application?	(7 13) That is, the cons of 7 onto the cons of 13 onto ( ).

What problem arises when we want
(vec+ *vec1* *vec2*), where
  vec1 is (3 7), and
  vec2 is (4 6 8 1)
	When *vec1* eventually gets to be ( ), we quit, but that means the final value will be (7 13), which is wrong. The final value should be (7 13 8 1).

Can we still write vec+ even if the vecs are not the same length?	Yes!

What trivial change can we make in the terminal condition line to get the correct final value?	Replace
	  ((null? *vec1*) (**quote** ( )))
	by
	  ((null? *vec1*) *vec2*).

What is (vec+ *vec1* *vec2*), where
  vec1 is (3 7 8 1), and
  vec2 is (4 6)
	No answer, since *vec2* will become null before *vec1*.
	  See The Fourth Commandment: We did not ask all the necessary questions!

What do we need to include in our function?	Another terminal condition.

What is the other terminal condition line?	((null? *vec2*) *vec1*).

So now that we have expanded our function definition so that vec+ works for any two vecs, see if you can rewrite it.

```
(define vec+
  (lambda (vec1 vec2)
    (cond
      ((null? vec1) vec2)
      ((null? vec2) vec1)
      (t (cons (+ (car vec1) (car vec2))
             (vec+
               (cdr vec1) (cdr vec2)))))))
```

Does the order of the two terminal conditions matter?	No.
Is t really the last question?	Yes, because either (null? *vec1*) or (null? *vec2*) is true if either one of them does not contain at least one number.

What is (> *n m*) where
  n is 12, and
  m is 13
	nil, that is, false.

What is (> *n m*) where
  n is 12, and
  m is 11
	t, that is, true.

On how many numbers do we have to recur?	Two, *n* and *m*.
How do we recur?	With (sub1 *n*) and (sub1 *m*).
When do we recur?	When we know that neither number is equal to 0.

| How many questions do we have to ask about n and m? | Three: (zero? n), (zero? m), and t. |

| Can you write the function $>$ now using zero?, add1, and sub1 | How about: |

```
(define >
  (lambda (n m)
    (cond
      ((zero? m) t)
      ((zero? n) nil)
      (t (> (sub1 n) (sub1 m))))))
```

| Is the way we wrote ($> n\ m$) correct? | No, try it for the case where n and m are the same number. Let n and m be 3. |

| (zero? m), where
  n is 3, and
  m is 3 | No, so move to the next question. |

| (zero? n), where
  n is 3, and
  m is 3 | No, so move to the next question. |

| What is the meaning of
  ($>$ (sub1 n) (sub1 m)) | Recur, but with *both* arguments reduced by one. |

| (zero? m), where
  n is 2, and
  m is 2 | No, so move to the next question. |

| (zero? n), where
  n is 2, and
  m is 2 | No, so move to the next question. |

What is the meaning of (> (sub1 *n*) (sub1 *m*))	Recur, but with *both* arguments closer to zero by one.

(zero? *m*), where
    n is 1, and
    m is 1
	No, so move to the next question.

(zero? *n*), where
    n is 1, and
    m is 1
	No, so move to the next question.

What is the meaning of (> (sub1 *n*) (sub1 *m*))	Recur, but with *both* arguments reduced by one.

(zero? *m*), where
    n is 0, and
    m is 0
	Yes, so the value of (> *n* *m*) is *t*.

Is this correct?	No, because 3 is **not** greater than 3.
How can we change the function > to take care of this subtle problem?	Switch the zero? lines, that is:

```
(define >
  (lambda (n m)
    (cond
      ((zero? n) nil)
      ((zero? m) t)
      (t (> (sub1 n) (sub1 m))))))
```

What is (< *n* *m*), where
    n is 4, and
    m is 6.
	t.

($<$ n m), where
  n is 8, and
  m is 3
	nil.

($<$ n m), where
  n is 6, and
  m is 6
	nil.

Now try to write $<$	**(define** $<$
	  (lambda (n m)
	    (cond
	      ((zero? m) nil)
	      ((zero? n) t)
	      (t ($<$ (sub1 n) (sub1 m))))))

Here is the definition of $=$

(define $=$
  (lambda (n m)
    (cond
      ((zero? m) (zero? n))
      ((zero? n) nil)
      (t ($=$ (sub1 n) (sub1 m)))))))

(define $=$
  (lambda (n m)
    (cond
      (($>$ n m) nil)
      (($<$ n m) nil)
      (t t))))

Rewrite $=$ using $<$ and $>$

Does this mean we have two different functions for testing equality of atoms?	Yes, they are $=$ for atoms which are numbers and eq? for the others.[1]

_____

[1] In practice, eq? does work for some numbers.

($\uparrow$ n m), where
  n is 1, and
  m is 1
	1

$(\uparrow\ n\ m)$, where
    n is 2, and
    m is 3
	8

$(\uparrow\ n\ m)$, where
    n is 5, and
    m is 3
	125

Now write the function $\uparrow$
    Hint: See the The Fourth and Fifth Commandments.
	(**define** $\uparrow$
	  (**lambda** $(n\ m)$
	    (**cond**
	      ((zero? m) 1)
	      (t ($\times$ n ($\uparrow$ n (sub1 m)))))))

What is the value of (length lat), where
    lat is (hotdogs with mustard sauerkraut
        and pickles)
	6

What is (length lat), where lat is (ham and cheese on rye)	5

Now try to write the function length.	(**define** length
	  (**lambda** (lat)
	    (**cond**
	      ((null? lat) 0)
	      (t (add1 (length (cdr lat)))))))

What is (pick n lat), where
    n is 4, and
    lat is (lasagna spaghetti ravioli
        macaroni meatball)
	macaroni.

What is (pick *n* *lat*), where *n* is 0, and *lat* is (a)	No answer.

What is (pick *n* *lat*), where *n* is 0, and *lat* is ( )?	Let's define one: *nil*.

Try to write the function pick.	<pre>(**define** pick
	  (**lambda** (*n* *lat*)
	    (**cond**
	      ((null? *lat*) nil)
	      ((zero? (sub1 *n*)) (car *lat*))
	      (t (pick (sub1 *n*) (cdr *lat*))))))</pre>

Does the order of the two terminal conditions matter?	Think about it.

Does the order of the two terminal conditions matter?	Try it out!

Does the order of the two previous answers matter?	Yes. Think first, then try.

What is (rempick *n* *lat*), where *n* is 3, and *lat* is (hotdogs with hot mustard)	(hotdogs with mustard).

What is (rempick *n* *lat*), where *n* is 0, and *lat* is ( )	Let's define an answer: ( ).

Now try to write rempick.

```
(define rempick
  (lambda (n lat)
    (cond
      ((null? lat) (quote ( )))
      ((zero? (sub1 n)) (cdr lat))
      (t (cons (car lat)
           (rempick
             (sub1 n) (cdr lat)))))))
```

Is (number?[1] a) true or false, where
   a is tomato

False.

---

[1] L: numberp

Is (number? a) true or false, where
   a is 76

True.

Can you write number?, which is true if its
argument is a numeric atom and false if its
argument is a non-numeric atom?

No. number?, like add1, sub1, zero?, car,
cdr, cons, null?, eq? and atom?, is a primitive function.

Now, using number?, write a function
no-nums, which gives as a final value a lat
obtained by removing all the numbers from
the lat. For example, where lat is
   (5 pears 6 prunes 9 dates),
(no-nums lat) is
   (pears prunes dates).

```
(define no-nums
  (lambda (lat)
    (cond
      ((null? lat) (quote ( )))
      (t (cond
           ((number? (car lat))
            (no-nums (cdr lat)))
           (t (cons (car lat)
                (no-nums (cdr lat)))))))))
```

Now write all-nums which builds a vec as a final value given a lat.

```
(define all-nums
  (lambda (lat)
    (cond
      ((null? lat) (quote ( )))
      (t (cond
           ((number? (car lat))
            (cons (car lat)
              (all-nums (cdr lat))))
           (t (all-nums (cdr lat)))))))))
```

Write the function eqan? which is true if its two arguments, *a1* and *a2*, are the same atom. Remember to use = for numbers and eq? for all others.

```
(define eqan?
  (lambda (a1 a2)
    (cond
      ((number? a1)
       (cond
         ((number? a2) (= a1 a2))
         (t nil)))
      ((number? a2) nil)
      (t (eq? a1 a2)))))
```

Can we assume that all functions written using eq? can be generalized by replacing eq? by eqan?

Yes, except of course, for eqan? itself.

Wouldn't a (ham and cheese on rye) be good right now?

Don't forget the mustard!

Exercises

For these exercises,

$$vec1 \text{ is } (1\ 2)$$
$$vec2 \text{ is } (3\ 2\ 4)$$
$$vec3 \text{ is } (2\ 1\ 3)$$
$$vec4 \text{ is } (6\ 2\ 1)$$
$$l \text{ is } (\ )$$
$$zero \text{ is } 0$$
$$one \text{ is } 1$$
$$three \text{ is } 3$$
$$obj \text{ is } (x\ y)$$

4.1 Write the function duplicate of *n* and *obj* which builds a list containing *n* objects *obj*.
Example: (duplicate *three obj*) is ((x y) (x y) (x y)),
        (duplicate *zero obj*) is ( ),
      (duplicate *one vec1*) is ((1 2)).

4.2 Write the function multvec that builds a number by multiplying all the numbers in a vec.
Example: (multvec *vec2*) is 24,
        (multvec *vec3*) is 6,
          (multvec *l*) is 1.

4.3 When building a value with ↑, which value should you use for the terminal line?

4.4 Argue the correctness for the function ↑ as we did for ($\times$ *n m*). Use 3 and 4 as data.

4.5 Write the function index of *a* and *lat* that returns the place of the atom *a* in *lat*. You may assume that *a* is a member of *lat*. Hint: Can *lat* be empty?

Example: When *a* is car,

        lat1 is (cons cdr car null? eq?),

          b is motor, and

        lat2 is (car engine auto motor),

we have (index *a lat1*) is 3,

      (index *a lat2*) is 1,

      (index *b lat2*) is 4.

4.6 Write the function product of *vec1* and *vec2* that multiplies corresponding numbers in *vec1* and *vec2* and builds a new *vec* from the results. The vecs, *vec1* and *vec2*, may differ in length.

Example: (product *vec1 vec2*) is (3 4 4),

      (product *vec2 vec3*) is (6 2 12),

      (product *vec3 vec4*) is (12 2 3).

4.7 Write the function dot-product of *vec1* and *vec2* that multiplies corresponding numbers in *vec1* and *vec2* and builds a new *number* by summing the results. The vecs, *vec1* and *vec2*, are the same length.

Example: (dot-product *vec2 vec2*) is 29,

      (dot-product *vec2 vec4*) is 26,

      (dot-product *vec3 vec4*) is 17.

4.8 Write the function / that divides nonnegative integers.

Example: (/ *n m*) is 1, when *n* is 7 and *m* is 5.

      (/ *n m*) is 4, when *n* is 8 and *m* is 2.

      (/ *n m*) is 0, when *n* is 2 and *m* is 3.

Hint: A number is now defined as a rest (between 0 and $m - 1$) and a multiple addition of *m*. The number of additions is the result.

4.9 Here is the function remainder:

```
(define remainder
  (lambda (n m)
    (cond
      (t (− n (× m (/ n m)))))))
```

Make up examples for the application (remainder *n m*) and work through them.

4.10 Write the function ≤ which tests if two numbers are equal or if the first is less than the second.

Example: (≤ *zero one*) is true,

        (≤ *one one*) is true,

        (≤ *three one*) is false.

Chapter 5

The Multichapter Chapter

Write the function member?

```
(define member?
  (lambda (a lat)
    (cond
      ((null? lat) nil)
      (t (or
           (eq? (car lat) a)
           (member? a (cdr lat)))))))
```

Do you recall, or can you see now, what member? does?

It checks each atom of the lat to see if it is the same as the atom *a*. When it finds the first occurrence of *a*, it stops and returns *t*.

Write the function rember.

```
(define rember
  (lambda (a lat)
    (cond
      ((null? lat) (quote ( )))
      (t (cond
           ((eq? (car lat) a) (cdr lat))
           (t (cons (car lat)
                (rember
                  a (cdr lat)))))))))
```

Do you recall, or can you see now, what rember does?

Rember looks at each atom of the lat to see if it is the same as the atom *a*. If it is not, rember saves the atom and proceeds. When it finds the first occurrence of *a*, it stops and gives the value (cdr *lat*), or the rest of the lat, so that the value returned is the original lat, with only the first occurrence of *a* removed.

Write the function multirember which gives as its final value the lat with *all* occurrences of *a* removed.

```
(define multirember
  (lambda (a lat)
    (cond
      ( _____  _____ )
      (t (cond
           ( _____  _____ )
           ( _____  _____ ))))))
```

Hint: What do we want as the value when
  (eq? (car *lat*) *a*) is true?
Consider the example where
  a is cup, and
  lat is (coffee cup tea cup and hick cup).

```
(define multirember
  (lambda (a lat)
    (cond
      ((null? lat) (quote ( )))
      (t (cond
           ((eq? (car lat) a)
            (multirember a (cdr lat)))
           (t (cons (car lat)
                (multirember
                  a (cdr lat)))))))))
```

After the first occurrence of *a*, we now recur with (multirember *a* (cdr *lat*)), in order to remove the other occurrences.

The value of the application is
  (coffee tea and hick).

Can you see how multirember works?

Possibly not, so we will go through the steps necessary to arrive at the value
  (coffee tea and hick).

(null? *lat*)

No, so move to the next line.

---

t

t.

(eq? (car *lat*) *a*)

No, so move to the next line.

What is the meaning of
  (cons
    (car *lat*)
    (multirember *a* (cdr *lat*)))

Save (car *lat*), namely **coffee**, to be cons*ed* onto the value of (multirember *a* (cdr *lat*)) later. Now determine
  (multirember *a* (cdr *lat*)).

(null? *lat*)

No, so move to the next line.

---

t	t.
(eq? (car *lat*) *a*)	Yes, so forget (car *lat*), and determine (multirember *a* (cdr *lat*)).
(null? *lat*)	No, so move to the next line.
t	Yes!
(eq? (car *lat*) *a*)	No, so move to the next line.

What is the meaning of
  (cons
    (car *lat*)
    (multirember *a* (cdr *lat*)))
	Save (car *lat*), namely **tea**, to be cons*ed* onto the value of (multirember *a* (cdr *lat*)) later. Now determine
	  (multirember *a* (cdr *lat*)).

(null? *lat*)	No, so move to the next line.
t	t.
(eq? (car *lat*) *a*)	Yes, so forget (car *lat*), and determine (multirember *a* (cdr *lat*)).
(null? *lat*)	No, so move to the next line.
(eq? (car *lat*) *a*)	No, so move to the next line.

What is the meaning of
  (cons
    (car *lat*)
    (multirember *a* (cdr *lat*)))
	Save (car *lat*), namely and, to be cons*ed*
	onto the value of (multirember *a* (cdr *lat*))
	later. Now determine
	    (multirember *a* (cdr *lat*)).

(null? *lat*)	No, so move to the next line.
(eq? (car *lat*) *a*)	No, so move to the next line.

What is the meaning of
  (cons
    (car *lat*)
    (multirember *a* (cdr *lat*)))
	Save (car *lat*), namely hick, to be cons*ed*
	onto the value of (multirember *a* (cdr *lat*))
	later. Now determine
	    (multirember *a* (cdr *lat*)).

(null? *lat*)	No, so move to the next line.
(eq? (car *lat*) *a*)	Yes, so forget (car *lat*), and determine (multirember *a* (cdr *lat*)).
(null? *lat*)	Yes, so we have a value of ( ).
Are we finished?	No. We still have several cons*es* to pick up.
What do we do next?	We cons the most recent (car *lat*) we have, namely hick, onto ( ).
What do we do next?	We cons and onto (hick).
What do we do next?	We cons tea onto (and hick).

What do we do next?

We cons coffee onto (tea and hick).

Are we finished now?

Yes.

Now write the function multiinsertR.

```
(define multiinsertR
  (lambda (new old lat)
    (cond
      ( _____  _____ )
      (t (cond
           ( _____  _____ )
           ( _____  _____ )))))))
```

```
(define multiinsertR
  (lambda (new old lat)
    (cond
      ((null? lat) (quote ( )))
      (t (cond
           ((eq? (car lat) old)
            (cons (car lat)
              (cons new
                (multiinsertR
                  new old (cdr lat)))))
           (t (cons (car lat)
                (multiinsertR
                  new old (cdr lat)))))))))
```

It would also be correct to use *old* in place of (car *lat*) because we know that (eq? (car *lat*) *old*).

Is this function defined correctly?

```
(define multiinsertL
  (lambda (new old lat)
    (cond
      ((null? lat) (quote ( )))
      (t (cond
           ((eq? (car lat) old)
            (cons new
              (cons old
                (multiinsertL
                  new old lat))))
           (t (cons
                (car lat)
                (multiinsertL
                  new old (cdr lat)))))))))
```

Not quite. To find out why, go through the function, where

   new is fried,
   old is fish, and
   lat is (chips and fish or fish and fried).

Was the terminal condition ever reached?

No, because we never get past the first occurrence of *old*.

Now try to write the function multiinsertL:

```
(define multiinsertL
  (lambda (new old lat)
    (cond
      ( _____  _____ )
      (t (cond
           ( _____  _____ )
           ( _____  _____ )))))))
```

```
(define multiinsertL
  (lambda (new old lat)
    (cond
      ((null? lat) (quote ( )))
      (t (cond
           ((eq? (car lat) old)
            (cons new
              (cons old
                (multiinsertL
                  new old (cdr lat)))))
           (t (cons (car lat)
                (multiinsertL
                  new old (cdr lat)))))))))
```

Now write the function multisubst.

```
(define multisubst
  (lambda (new old lat)
    (cond
      ( _____  _____ )
      (t (cond
           ( _____  _____ )
           ( _____  _____ ))))))
```

```
(define multisubst
  (lambda (new old lat)
    (cond
      ((null? lat) (quote ( )))
      (t (cond
           ((eq? (car lat) old)
            (cons new
              (multisubst
                new old (cdr lat))))
           (t (cons (car lat)
              (multisubst
                new old (cdr lat))))))))))
```

Now write the function occur which counts the number of times an atom *a* appears in a *lat*.

```
(define occur
  (lambda (a lat)
    (cond
      ( _____  _____ )
      (t (cond
           ( _____  _____ )
           ( _____  _____ ))))))
```

```
(define occur
  (lambda (a lat)
    (cond
      ((null? lat) 0)
      (t (cond
           ((eq? (car lat) a)
            (add1 (occur a (cdr lat))))
           (t (occur a (cdr lat))))))))
```

Write the function one? where (one? n) is t if n is 1, and false (i.e., *nil*) otherwise.

```
(define one?
  (lambda (n)
    (cond
      ((zero? n) nil)
      (t (zero? (sub1 n))))))
```

or

```
(define one?
  (lambda (n)
    (cond
      (t (= n 1)))))
```

Guess how we can further simplify this function, making it a *one-liner*.

By removing the (**cond** clause, we get

```
(define one?
  (lambda (n)
    (= n 1)))
```

Now rewrite the function rempick that removes the nth atom from the lat. For example, where

    n is 3, and

    lat is (lemon meringue salty pie).

the application (rempick n *lat*) has the value

    (lemon meringue pie).

Use the function one? in your answer.

```
(define rempick
  (lambda (n lat)
    (cond
      ((null? lat) (quote ( )))
      ((one? n) (cdr lat))
      (t (cons (car lat)
           (rempick
             (sub1 n) (cdr lat)))))))
```

Is rempick a "multi" function?

No.

Exercises

For these exercises,

x is comma
y is dot
a is kiwis
b is plums
lat1 is (bananas kiwis)
lat2 is (peaches apples bananas)
lat3 is (kiwis pears plums bananas cherries)
lat4 is (kiwis mangoes kiwis guavas kiwis)
l1 is ((curry) ( ) (chicken) ( ))
l2 is ((peaches) (and cream))
l3 is ((plums) and (ice) and cream)
l4 is ( )

5.1 For Exercise 3.4 you wrote the function subst-cake. Write the function multisubst-kiwis.
Example: (multisubst-kiwis *b lat1*) is (bananas plums),
(multisubst-kiwis *y lat2*) is (peaches apples bananas),
(multisubst-kiwis *y lat4*) is (dot mangoes dot guavas dot),
(multisubst-kiwis *y l4*) is ( ).

5.2 Write the function multisubst2. You can find subst2 at the end of Chapter 3.
Example: (multisubst2 *x a b lat1*) is (bananas comma),
(multisubst2 *y a b lat3*) is (dot pears dot bananas cherries),
(multisubst2 *a x y lat1*) is (bananas kiwis).

5.3 Write the function multidown of *lat* which replaces every atom in *lat* by a list containing the atom.
Example: (multidown *lat1*) is ((bananas) (kiwis)),
(multidown *lat2*) is ((peaches) (apples) (bananas)),
(multidown *l4*) is ( ).

5.4 Write the function occurN of *alat* and *lat* which counts how many times an atom in *alat* also occurs in *lat*.

Example: (occurN *lat1* *l4*) is 0,
(occurN *lat1* *lat2*) is 1,
(occurN *lat1* *lat3*) is 2.

5.5 The function I of *lat1* and *lat2* returns the first atom in *lat2* that is in both *lat1* and *lat2*. Write the functions I and multiI. multiI returns a list of atoms common to *lat1* and *lat2*.

Example: (I *lat1* *l4*) is ( ),
(I *lat1* *lat2*) is bananas,
(I *lat1* *lat3*) is kiwis;
(multiI *lat1* *l4*) is ( ),
(multiI *lat1* *lat2*) is (bananas),
(multiI *lat1* *lat3*) is (kiwis bananas).

5.6 Consider the following alternative definition of one?

```
(define one?
  (lambda (n)
    (cond
      ((zero? (sub1 n)) t)
      (t nil))))
```

Which Laws and/or Commandments does it violate?

5.7 Consider the following definition of =

```
(define =
  (lambda (n m)
    (cond
      ((zero? n) (zero? m))
      (t (= n (sub1 m))))))
```

This definition violates The Sixth Commandment. Why?

5.8 The function count0 of *vec* counts the number of zero elements in *vec*. What is wrong with the following definition? Can you fix it?

```
(define count0
  (lambda (vec)
    (cond
       ((null? vec) 1)
       (t (cond
             ((zero? (car vec))
              (cons 0 (count0 (cdr vec))))
             (t (count0 (cdr vec)))))))))
```

5.9 Write the function multiup of *l* which replaces every lat of length one in *l* by the atom in that list, and which also removes every empty list.

Example: (multiup *l4*) is ( ),

               (multiup *l1*) is (curry chicken),

               (multiup *l2*) is (peaches (and cream)).

5.10 Review all the Laws and Commandments. Check the functions in Chapters 4 and 5 to see if they obey the Commandments. When did we not obey them literally? Did we act according to their spirit?

But answer came there none—
* And this was scarcely odd, because*
They'd eaten every one.

The Walrus and The Carpenter
          —Lewis Carroll

Chapter 6

Oh My Gawd:
It's Full of Stars

True or false, (not (atom? *s*)), where   *t.*
    s is (hungarian goulash)

(not (atom? *s*)), where   *nil.*
    s is atom

(not (atom? *s*)), where   *t.* Do you get the idea?
    s is (turkish ((coffee) and) baklava)

What is (leftmost *l*), where   hot.
    l is ((hot) (tuna (and)) cheese)

(lat? *l*), where   *nil.*
    l is ((hot) (tuna (and)) cheese)

Is (car *l*) an atom, where   No.
    l is ((hot) (tuna (and)) cheese)

What is (leftmost *l*), where   hamburger.
    l is (((hamburger) french)
        (fries (and a) coke))

What is (leftmost *l*), where   4
    l is ((((4) four)) 17 (seventeen))

Now see if you can write the function
leftmost:

```
(define leftmost
  (lambda (l)
    (cond
      (_____  _____)
      (_____  _____)
      (_____  _____))))
```

```
(define leftmost
  (lambda (l)
    (cond
      ((null? l) (quote ( )))
      ((non-atom? (car l))
       (leftmost (car l)))
      (t (car l)))))
```

Using arguments from one of our previous
examples, follow through this to see how
it works. Notice that now we are recurring
down the *car* of the list, instead of the *cdr* of
the list.

What is (leftmost *l*), where
  l is (((( ) four)) 17 (seventeen))

( ).

Write non-atom?[1]

```
(define non-atom?
  (lambda (s)
    (not (atom? s))))
```

---

[1]   L: consp
      S: pair?

Write not.

```
(define not
  (lambda (b)
    (cond
      (b nil)
      (t t))))
```

What is (rember* *a* *l*), where
  a is cup, and
  l is ((coffee) cup ((tea) cup)
       (and (hick)) cup)
  "rember*" is pronounced "rember-star."

((coffee) ((tea)) (and (hick))).

What is (rember* *a l*), where
  a is sauce, and
  l is (((tomato sauce))
      ((bean) sauce)
      (and ((flying)) sauce))

(((tomato))
 ((bean))
 (and ((flying)))).

Now write rember*.[†]

```
(define rember*
  (lambda (a l)
    (cond
      ((null? l) (quote ( )))
      ((non-atom? (car l))
       (cons
         (rember* a (car l))
         (rember* a (cdr l))))
      (t (cond
           ((eq? (car l) a)
            (rember* a (cdr l)))
           (t (cons (car l)
                (rember* a (cdr l)))))))))
```

[†] "*" makes us think "oh my gawd."

What is (insertR* *new old l*), where
  new is roast,
  old is chuck, and
  l is ((how much (wood))
     could
     ((a (wood) chuck))
     (((chuck)))
     (if (a) ((wood chuck)))
     could chuck wood)

((how much (wood))
 could
 ((a (wood) chuck roast))
 (((chuck roast)))
 (if (a) ((wood chuck roast)))
 could chuck roast wood).

Now write the function insertR* which inserts the atom *new* to the right of *old*, regardless of where *old* occurs.

```
(define insertR*
  (lambda (new old l)
    (cond
      ( _____ _____ )
      ( _____ _____ )
      ( _____ _____ )))))
```

```
(define insertR*
  (lambda (new old l)
    (cond
      ((null? l) (quote ( )))
      ((non-atom? (car l))
       (cons
         (insertR* new old (car l))
         (insertR* new old (cdr l))))
      (t (cond
           ((eq? (car l) old)
            (cons old
              (cons new
                (insertR*
                  new old (cdr l)))))
           (t (cons (car l)
                (insertR*
                  new old (cdr l)))))))))))
```

How are insertR* and leftmost similar?	Both functions recur with the car when the car is a non-null list.
How are rember* and multirember different?	Multirember does not recur with the car. Rember* recurs with the car as well as with the cdr. It does not recur with the car, however, until it finds out that the car is a non-null list.
How are insertR* and rember* similar?	They both recur with the car, whenever the car is a non-null list, as well as with the cdr.
How are *all* *-functions similar?	They *all* recur with the car as well as with the cdr, whenever the car is a non-null list.

Why?	Because all ∗-functions work on general lists which are either
	— empty,
	— a non-null list cons*ed* onto a list, or
	— an atom cons*ed* onto a list.

The Fourth Commandment

(revised)

When recurring on a list of atoms, *lat*, or a vec, *vec*, ask two questions about them, and use (cdr *lat*) or (cdr *vec*) for the natural recursion.

When recurring on a list of S-expressions, *l*, ask three questions: (null? *l*), (atom? (car *l*)), and (non-atom? (car *l*)); and use (car *l*) and (cdr *l*) for the natural recursion.

When recurring on a number, *n*, ask two questions, and use (sub1 *n*) for the natural recursion.

(occursomething *a l*), where
    a is banana, and
    l is ((banana)
        (split ((((banana ice)))
                (cream (banana))
                sherbet))
        (banana)
        (bread)
        (banana brandy))
	5

What is a better function name for occursomething	occur∗.

Write occur*

```
(define occur*
  (lambda (a l)
    (cond
      (_____  _____ )
      (_____  _____ )
      (_____  _____ ))))
```

```
(define occur*
  (lambda (a l)
    (cond
      ((null? l) 0)
      ((non-atom? (car l))
       (+ (occur* a (car l))
          (occur* a (cdr l))))
      (t (cond
           ((eq? (car l) a)
            (add1 (occur* a (cdr l))))
           (t (occur* a (cdr l)))))))))
```

(subst* *new old l*), where
  new is orange,
  old is banana, and
  l is ((banana)
      (split ((((banana ice)))
           (cream (banana))
           sherbet))
      (banana)
      (bread)
      (banana brandy))

((orange)
(split ((((orange ice)))
    (cream (orange))
    sherbet))
(orange)
(bread)
(orange brandy)).

Write subst*

```
(define subst*
  (lambda (new old l)
    (cond
      ( _____  _____ )
      ( _____  _____ )
      ( _____  _____ )))))
```

```
(define subst*
  (lambda (new old l)
    (cond
      ((null? l) (quote ( )))
      ((non-atom? (car l))
       (cons
         (subst* new old (car l))
         (subst* new old (cdr l))))
      (t (cond
           ((eq? (car l) old)
            (cons new
              (subst* new old (cdr l))))
           (t (cons (car l)
                (subst*
                  new old (cdr l)))))))))))
```

What is (insertL* new old l), where
  new is pecker,
  old is chuck, and
  l is ((how much (wood))
      could
      ((a (wood) chuck))
      (((chuck)))
      (if (a) ((wood chuck)))
      could chuck wood)

((how much (wood))
could
((a (wood) pecker chuck))
(((pecker chuck)))
(if (a) ((wood pecker chuck)))
could pecker chuck wood).

Write insertL*:

```
(define insertL*
  (lambda (new old l)
    (cond
      (_____ _____ )
      (_____ _____ )
      (_____ _____ ))))
```

(**define** insertL*
  (**lambda** (*new old l*)
    (**cond**
      ((null? *l*) (**quote** ( )))
      ((non-atom? (car *l*))
      (cons
        (insertL* *new old* (car *l*))
        (insertL* *new old* (cdr *l*))))
      (t (**cond**
        ((eq? (car *l*) *old*)
        (cons *new*
          (cons *old*
            (insertL*
              new old (cdr *l*)))))
        (t (cons (car *l*)
          (insertL*
            new old (cdr *l*)))))))))))

(member* *a l*), where
  a is chips, and
  l is ((potato) (chips ((with) fish) (chips)))

t, because the atom chips appears in the list *l*.

Write member*:

```
(define member*
  (lambda (a l)
    (cond
      (_____ _____ )
      (_____ _____ )
      (_____ _____ ))))
```

(**define** member*
  (**lambda** (*a l*)
    (**cond**
      ((null? *l*) nil)
      ((non-atom? (car *l*))
      (**or**
        (member* *a* (car *l*))
        (member* *a* (cdr *l*))))
      (t (**or**
        (eq? (car *l*) *a*)
        (member* *a* (cdr *l*))))))))

What is (member* *a l*), where
  a is chips, and
  l is ((potato) (chips ((with) fish) (chips)))
	t.

Which chips did it find?	((potato) (<u>chips</u> ((with) fish) (chips))).

Try to write member* without using non-atom?

```
(define member*
  (lambda (a l)
    (cond
      ((null? l) nil)
      ((atom? (car l))
       (or
         (eq? (car l) a)
         (member* a (cdr l))))
      (t (or
           (member* a (car l))
           (member* a (cdr l)))))))
```

Do you remember what (**or** ...) does?	(**or** ...) asks questions one at a time until it finds one that is true. Then (**or** ...) stops, making its value true. If it cannot find a true argument, then the value of (**or** ...) is false.

What is
  (**and** (atom? (car *l*))
      (eq? (car *l*) *x*)),
where
  x is pizza, and
  l is (mozzarella pizza)
	nil.

Why is it false?	Since (**and** ...) asks (atom? (car *l*)), which is true, it then asks (eq? (car *l*) *x*), which is false; hence it is *nil.*

What is
  (**and** (atom? (car *l*))
      (eq? (car *l*) *x*)),
where
  x is pizza, and
  l is ((mozzarella mushroom) pizza)
	nil.

Why is it false?	Since (**and** ...) asks (atom? (car *l*)), and it is not; so it is *nil*.

Give an example for *x* and *l* where the expression is true.	Here's one:
	  x is pizza, and
	  l is (pizza (tastes good)).

Put in your own words what (**and** ...) does.	(**and** ...) asks questions one at a time until it finds an argument which is false. Then (**and** ...) stops with false. If it cannot find a false argument, then it is true.

True or false, it is possible that one of the arguments of (**and** ...) and (**or** ...) is not considered?[1]	True, because (**and** ...) stops if the first argument has the value *nil*, and (**or** ...) stops if the first argument has the value *t*.

---

[1] (**cond** ...) also has the property of not considering all of its arguments.

(eqlist? *l1 l2*), where
  l1 is (strawberry ice cream), and
  l2 is (strawberry ice cream)
	t.

(eqlist? *l1 l2*), where
  l1 is (strawberry ice cream), and
  l2 is (strawberry cream ice)
	nil.

(eqlist? *l1 l2*), where
    l1 is (banana ((split))), and
    l2 is ((banana) (split))
	nil.

(eqlist? *l1 l2*), where
    l1 is (beef ((sausage)) (and (soda))), and
    l2 is (beef ((salami)) (and (soda)))
	nil, but almost *t.*

(eqlist? *l1 l2*), where
    l1 is (beef ((sausage)) (and (soda))), and
    l2 is (beef ((sausage)) (and (soda)))
	t. That's better.

What is eqlist?	It is a function that determines if the two lists are structurally the same.

Write eqlist? using eqan?	

```
(define eqlist?
  (lambda (l1 l2)
    (cond
      ((and (null? l1) (null? l2)) t)
      ((or (null? l1) (null? l2)) nil)
      ((and (non-atom? (car l1))
            (non-atom? (car l2)))
       (and (eqlist? (car l1) (car l2))
            (eqlist? (cdr l1) (cdr l2))))
      ((or (non-atom? (car l1))
           (non-atom? (car l2))) nil)
      (t (and
           (eqan? (car l1) (car l2))
           (eqlist? (cdr l1) (cdr l2)))))))
```

Why is there no explicit test for atoms?	If we know that the car of each list is not a list, then the car of each list must be an atom.

Write the function equal? which determines if two S-expressions are structurally the same.

```
(define equal?
  (lambda (s1 s2)
    (cond
      ((and (atom? s1) (atom? s2))
       (eqan? s1 s2))
      ((and
         (non-atom? s1)
         (non-atom? s2))
       (eqlist? s1 s2))
      (t nil))))
```

Now, rewrite eqlist? using equal?

```
(define eqlist?
  (lambda (l1 l2)
    (cond
      ((and (null? l1) (null? l2)) t)
      ((or (null? l1) (null? l2)) nil)
      (t (and
           (equal? (car l1) (car l2))
           (eqlist? (cdr l1) (cdr l2)))))))
```

Is equal? a "star" function?

Yes.

How would rember change if we replaced *lat* by a general list *l* and if we replaced *a* by an arbitrary S-expression *s*?

```
(define rember
  (lambda (s l)
    (cond
      ((null? l) (quote ( )))
      ((non-atom? (car l))
       (cond
         ((equal? (car l) s) (cdr l))
         (t (cons (car l)
                  (rember s (cdr l))))))
      (t (cond
           ((equal? (car l) s) (cdr l))
           (t (cons (car l)
                    (rember s (cdr l)))))))))
```

And how does that differ?	Rember now removes the first matching S-expression *s* in the list *l*, instead of the first matching atom *a* in the lat *lat*.

Is rember a "star" function now?	No.

Why not?	Because rember only recurs with the (cdr *l*).

Can you simplify rember?

Obviously!

```
(define rember
  (lambda (s l)
    (cond
      ((null? l) (quote ( )))
      (t (cond
           ((equal? (car l) s) (cdr l))
           (t (cons (car l)
                (rember s (cdr l)))))))))
```

Can you simplify rember even more?	Yes, the inner (**cond** ...) is asking questions that the outer (**cond** ...) could ask!

Do it!

```
(define rember
  (lambda (s l)
    (cond
      ((null? l) (quote ( )))
      ((equal? (car l) s) (cdr l))
      (t (cons (car l)
           (rember s (cdr l)))))))
```

Simplify insertL*

```
(define insertL*
  (lambda (new old l)
    (cond
      ((null? l) (quote ( )))
      ((non-atom? (car l))
       (cons
         (insertL* new old (car l))
         (insertL* new old (cdr l))))
      ((eq? (car l) old)
       (cons new
         (cons old
           (insertL* new old (cdr l)))))
      (t (cons (car l)
           (insertL*
             new old (cdr l)))))))
```

Do these new definitions look simpler?

Yes, they do!

And they work just as well.

Yes, because we know that all the cases and recursions are right before we simplify.

The Seventh Commandment

Simplify only after the function is correct.

Can all functions that were written using eq? and = be generalized by replacing eq? and = by the function equal?

Not quite; this won't work for eqan?, but will work for all others. In fact, disregarding the trivial example of eqan?, that is exactly what we shall assume.

Exercises

For these exercises,

> *l1* is ((fried potatoes) (baked (fried)) tomatoes)
> *l2* is (((chili) chili (chili)))
> *l3* is ( )
> *lat1* is (chili and hot)
> *lat2* is (baked fried)
> *a* is fried

6.1 Write the function down* of *l* which puts every atom in *l* in a list by itself.

Example: (down* *l2*) is ((((chili)) (chili) ((chili)))),

   (down* *l3*) is ( ),

  (down* *lat1*) is ((chili) (and) (hot)).

6.2 Write the function occurN* of *lat* and *l* which counts all the atoms that are common to *lat* and *l*.

Example: (occurN* *lat1* *l2*) is 3,

   (occurN* *lat2* *l1*) is 3,

   (occurN* *lat1* *l3*) is 0.

6.3 Write the function double* of *a* and *l* which doubles each occurrence of *a* in *l*.

Example: (double* *a* *l1*) is ((fried fried potatoes) (baked (fried fried)) tomatoes),

   (double* *a* *l2*) is (((chili) chili (chili))),

  (double* *a* *lat2*) is (baked fried fried).

6.4 Consider the function lat? from Chapter 2. Argue why lat? has to ask three questions (and not two like the other functions in Chapter 2). Why does lat? not have to recur on the car?

6.5 Make sure that (member* *a* *l*), where

 a is chips and
 l is ((potato) (chips ((with) fish) (chips))),

really discovers the first chips. Can you change member* so that it finds the last chips first?

6.6 Write the function list+ which adds up all the numbers in a general list of numbers.

Example: When *l1* is ((1 (6 6 ( )))),
and *l2* is ((1 2 (3 6)) 1), then
(list+ *l1*) is 13,
(list+ *l2*) is 13,
(list+ *l3*) is 0.

6.7 Consider the following function g* of *lvec* and *acc*.

```
(define g*
  (lambda (lvec acc)
    (cond
      ((null? lvec) acc)
      ((atom? (car lvec))
       (g* (cdr lvec) (+ (car lvec) acc)))
      (t (g* (car lvec) (g* (cdr lvec) acc))))))
```

The function is always applied to a (general) list of numbers and 0. Make up examples and find out what the function does.

6.8 Consider the following function f* of *l* and *acc*.

```
(define f*
  (lambda (l acc)
    (cond
      ((null? l) acc)
      ((atom? (car l))
       (cond
         ((member? (car l) acc) (f* (cdr l) acc))
         (t (f* (cdr l) (cons (car l) acc)))))
      (t (f* (car l) (f* (cdr l) acc))))))
```

The function is always applied to a list and the empty list. Make up examples for *l* and step through the applications. Generalize in one sentence what f* does.

6.9 The functions in Exercises 6.7 and 6.8 employ the *accumulator technique*. This means that they pass along an argument that represents the result that has been computed so far. When these functions reach the bottom (null?, zero?), they just return the result contained in the accumulator. The original argument for the accumulator is the element that used to be the answer for the null?-case. Write the function occur (see Chapter 5) of *a* and *lat* using the accumulator technique. What is the original value for *acc*?

6.10 Step through an application of the original occur and the occur from Exercise 6.9 and compare the arguments in the recursive applications. Can you write occur* using the accumulator technique?

Have you taken a tea break yet?
We're taking ours now.

Chapter 7

Shadows

Is 1 an arithmetic expression?	Yes.
Is 3 an arithmetic expression?	Yes, of course.
Is 1 + 3 an arithmetic expression?	Yes!
Is 1 + 3 × 4 an arithmetic expression?	Definitely.
Is cookie an arithmetic expression?	Yes. Are you almost ready for one?
And, what about 3 ↑ y + 5	Yes.
What is an arithmetic expression in your words?	In ours: "For the purpose of this chapter, an arithmetic expression is either an atom (including numbers), or two arithmetic expressions combined by +, ×, or ↑."
What is (**quote** a)	a.
What is (**quote** +)	+.
What does (**quote** ×) stand for?	×.
And (**quote** (a b c))	(a b c).
Can you describe what (**quote** ...) does?	(**quote** ...) is a *special form* that returns as its value literally whatever it gets as an argument.

Is (eq? (**quote** a) x) true or false, where x is a	True.
Is (x + 3) an arithmetic expression?	Not really, since there are parentheses around x + 3. Our definition of arithmetic expression did not mention parentheses.
Could we think of (x + 3) as an arithmetic expression?	Yes, if we keep in mind that the parentheses are not really there.
What would you call (x + 3)	We call it a *representation* for x + 3.
Why is (x + 3) a good representation?	Because 1. (x + 3) is an S-expression. It can therefore serve as an argument for a function, and 2. It structurally resembles the expression we want to represent.
True or false, (numbered? x) where x is 1	True.
How do you represent $3 + 4 \times 5$	(3 + (4 × 5)).
True or false, (numbered? y) where y is (3 + (4 ↑ 5))	True.
True or false, (numbered? z) where z is (2 × sausage)	False, because **sausage** is not a number. It is a symbol.[1]

---

[1]   L: Determined by **symbolp**
     S: Determined by **symbol?**

What is numbered?	It is a function which determines whether a *representation* of an arithmetic expression only contains numbers besides the +, ×, and ↑.

Now you can write a skeleton for numbered?	(**define** numbered?
	   (**lambda** (*aexp*)
	     (**cond**
	       (_____ _____)
	       (_____ _____)
	       (_____ _____)
	       (_____ _____))))
	
	 is a good guess.

What is the first question?	(atom? *aexp*).

What is (eq? (car (cdr *aexp*)) (**quote** +))	It is the second question.

Can you guess the third one?	(eq? (car (cdr *aexp*)) (**quote** ×)) is perfect.

And you must know the fourth one.	(eq? (car (cdr *aexp*)) (**quote** ↑)), of course.

Should we ask another question about *aexp*?	No! So we could replace the previous question by t.

Why do we ask not two but four questions about arithmetic expressions? After all, arithmetic expressions like (1 + 3) are lats.	Because we consider (1 + 3) as a representation of an arithmetic expression in list form, not as a list itself. And, an arithmetic expression is either a number, or two arithmetic expressions combined by +, ×, or ↑.

Now you can almost write numbered?	Here is our proposal:

```
(define numbered?
  (lambda (aexp)
    (cond
      ((atom? aexp) (number? aexp))
      ((eq? (car (cdr aexp)) (quote +))
       _____ )
      ((eq? (car (cdr aexp)) (quote ×))
       _____ )
      ((eq? (car (cdr aexp)) (quote ↑))
       _____ ))))
```

Why do we ask (number? *aexp*) when we know that *aexp* is an atom?	Because we want to know if all arithmetic expressions that are atoms are numbers.
What do we need to know if the *aexp* consists of two arithmetic expressions combined by +	We need to find out whether the two subexpressions are numbered.
In which position is the first subexpression?	It is the car of *aexp*.
In which position is the second subexpression?	It is the car of the cdr of the cdr of *aexp*.
So what do we need to ask?	(numbered? (car *aexp*)) and (numbered? (car (cdr (cdr *aexp*)))). Both questions must be true.
What is the second question?	(**and** (numbered? (car *aexp*)) (numbered? (car (cdr (cdr *aexp*)))))).

Try numbered? again.

```
(define numbered?
  (lambda (aexp)
    (cond
      ((atom? aexp) (number? aexp))
      ((eq? (car (cdr aexp)) (quote +))
       (and
         (numbered? (car aexp))
         (numbered?
           (car (cdr (cdr aexp))))))
      ((eq? (car (cdr aexp)) (quote ×))
       (and
         (numbered? (car aexp))
         (numbered?
           (car (cdr (cdr aexp))))))
      ((eq? (car (cdr aexp)) (quote ↑))
       (and
         (numbered? (car aexp))
         (numbered?
           (car (cdr (cdr aexp)))))))))
```

Since *aexp* is known to be an arithmetic expression, could we have written numbered? in a simpler way?

Yes:

```
(define numbered?
  (lambda (aexp)
    (cond
      ((atom? aexp) (number? aexp))
      (t (and
           (numbered? (car aexp))
           (numbered?
             (car (cdr (cdr aexp)))))))))
```

Why can we simplify?

Because we know we've got the function right.

What is (value *u*) where
  u is 13

13

(value x) where x is $(1 + 3)$	4
(value y) where y is $(1 + (3 \uparrow 4))$	82
(value z) where z is cookie	No answer.
(value $aexp$) returns what we think is the *natural value* of a numbered arithmetic expression.	We hope.
How many questions will value ask about *aexp*?	Four.

Now, let's write a first attempt at value.	```
	(define value
	  (lambda (aexp)
	    (cond
	      ((number? aexp)
	       _____)
	      ((eq? (car (cdr aexp)) (quote +))
	       _____)
	      ((eq? (car (cdr aexp)) (quote ×))
	       _____)
	      (t _____))))
	``

What is the natural value of an arithmetic expression that is a number?	It is just that number.
What is the natural value of an arithmetic expression that consists of two arithmetic expressions combined by +	If we had the natural value of the two subexpressions, we could just add up the two values.

Can you think of a way to get the value of the two subexpressions in (1 + (3 × 4))

Of course, by applying value to 1, and to (3 × 4).

And in general?

By recurring with value on the subexpressions.

The Eighth Commandment

Recur on all the *subparts* that are of the same nature:

—On all the sublists of a list.

—On all the subexpressions of a representation of an arithmetic expression.

Give value another try.

```
(define value
  (lambda (aexp)
    (cond
      ((number? aexp) aexp)
      ((eq? (car (cdr aexp)) (quote +))
       (+ (value (car aexp))
          (value (car (cdr (cdr aexp))))))
      ((eq? (car (cdr aexp)) (quote ×))
       (× (value (car aexp))
          (value (car (cdr (cdr aexp))))))
      (t (↑ (value (car aexp))
            (value
              (car (cdr (cdr aexp)))))))))
```

Can you think of a different representation of arithmetic expressions?

There are several of them.

Could (3 4 +) represent 3 + 4	Yes.
Could (+ 3 4)	Yes.
Or (plus 3 4)	Yes.
Is (plus (times 3 6) (expt 8 2)) a representation of an arithmetic expression?	Yes.

Try to write the function value for a new kind of arithmetic expression that is either: — a number — a list of the atom **plus** followed by two arithmetic expressions — a list of the atom **times** followed by two arithmetic expressions — or, a list of the atom **expt** followed by two arithmetic expressions.	What about (**define** value 　(**lambda** (*aexp*) 　　(**cond** 　　　((number? *aexp*) *aexp*) 　　　((eq? (car *aexp*) (**quote** plus)) 　　　　(+ (value (cdr *aexp*)) 　　　　　(value (cdr (cdr *aexp*))))) 　　　((eq? (car *aexp*) (**quote** times)) 　　　　(× (value (cdr *aexp*)) 　　　　　(value (cdr (cdr *aexp*))))) 　　　(t (↑ (value (cdr *aexp*)) 　　　　　(value (cdr (cdr *aexp*)))))))))

You guessed it.	It's wrong.
Let's try an example:	(plus 1 3).
(number? *aexp*), where 　*aexp* is (plus 1 3)	No.

(eq? (car *aexp*) (**quote** plus)), where *aexp* is (plus 1 3)	Yes.
And now recur.	Yes.
What is (cdr *aexp*), where *aexp* is (plus 1 3)	(1 3).
(1 3) is not our representation of an arithmetic expression.	No, we violated The Eighth Commandment. (1 3) is not a subpart that is a representation of an arithmetic expression! We obviously recurred on a *list*. But remember, not all lists are representations of arithmetic expressions. We have to recur on subexpressions.
How can we get the first subexpression of a representation of an arithmetic expression?	By taking the car of the cdr.
Is (cdr (cdr *aexp*)) an arithmetic expression where *aexp* is (plus 1 3)	No, the cdr of the cdr is (3), and (3) is not an arithmetic expression.
Again, we were thinking of the list (plus 1 3) instead of the representation for an arithmetic expression.	Taking the car of the cdr of the cdr gets us back on the right track.
What do we mean if we say the car of the cdr of *aexp*?	The first subexpression of the representation of an arithmetic expression.

Let's write a function 1st-sub-exp for arithmetic expressions.	(**define** 1st-sub-exp
	  (**lambda** (*aexp*)
	    (**cond**
	      (t (car (cdr *aexp*))))))

Why do we ask t?	Because the first question is also the last question.

Can we get by without (**cond** ...) if we don't need to ask questions?	Yes, remember one-liners.
	
	(**define** 1st-sub-exp
	  (**lambda** (*aexp*)
	    (car (cdr *aexp*))))

Write 2nd-sub-exp for arithmetic expressions.	(**define** 2nd-sub-exp
	  (**lambda** (*aexp*)
	    (car (cdr (cdr *aexp*)))))

Finally, let's replace (car *aexp*) by (operator *aexp*)	(**define** operator
	  (**lambda** (*aexp*)
	    (car *aexp*)))

Now write value again.

```
(define value
  (lambda (aexp)
    (cond
      ((number? aexp) aexp)
      ((eq? (operator aexp)
            (quote plus))
       (+ (value (1st-sub-exp aexp))
          (value (2nd-sub-exp aexp))))
      ((eq? (operator aexp)
            (quote times))
       (× (value (1st-sub-exp aexp))
          (value (2nd-sub-exp aexp))))
      (t (↑ (value (1st-sub-exp aexp))
            (value (2nd-sub-exp aexp)))))))))
```

Can we use this value function for the first representation of arithmetic expressions in this chapter?

Yes, by changing 1st-sub-exp and operator.

Do it!

```
(define 1st-sub-exp
  (lambda (aexp)
    (car aexp)))
```

```
(define operator
  (lambda (aexp)
    (car (cdr aexp))))
```

Wasn't this easy?

Yes, because we used help functions to hide the representation.

The Ninth Commandment

Use help functions to abstract from representations.

Have we seen representations before?	Yes, we just did not tell you that they were representations.
For what entities have we used representations?	Truth-values! Numbers!
Numbers are representations?	Yes. For example 4 stands for the concept four. We chose that symbol because we are accustomed to arabic representations.
What else could we have used?	(( ) ( ) ( ) ( )) would have served just as well. What about ((((( ))))))? How about (I V)?
Do you remember how many primitives we need for numbers?	Four: number?, zero?, add1, and sub1.
Let's try another representation for numbers. How shall we represent zero now?	( ) is our choice.
How is one represented?	(( )).
How is two represented?	(( ) ( )).
Got it? What's three?	Three is (( ) ( ) ( )).
Write a function to test for the null list.	(**define** null? (**lambda** (*s*) (**and** (atom? *s*) (eq? *s* (**quote** ( ))))))

Write a function to test for zero.	**(define** zero?
	  (lambda (n)
	    (null? n)))

Can you write add1	**(define** add1
	  (lambda (n)
	    (cons (**quote** ( )) n)))

What about sub1	**(define** sub1
	  (lambda (n)
	    (cdr n)))

Is this correct?	Let's see.

What is (sub1 n) where n is ( )	No answer, but that's fine. — Recall The Law of Cdr.

Rewrite + using this representation.	**(define** +
	  (lambda (n m)
	    (cond
	      ((zero? m) n)
	      (t (add1 (+ n (sub1 m))))))))

Has the definition of + changed?	No, only the definitions of its help functions (i.e., zero?, add1, and sub1) have changed.

How do we define a number in general?	A number is either zero or it is one added to a number.

How many questions do we need to ask in order to write number?	Two.

What is used in the natural recursion for number?	(cdr *n*).

| Write the function number? | ```
(define number?
  (lambda (n)
    (cond
      ((null? n) t)
      (t (and
           (null? (car n))
           (number? (cdr n)))))))
``` |

Is (cookie) a number in our representation?	No, but you deserve one now!

Go and get one!
```

Or better yet, make your own.

```
(define cookies
   (lambda ( )
      (bake
            (quote (350 degrees))
            (quote (12 minutes))
            (mix
                 (quote (walnuts 1 cup))
                 (quote (chocolate-chips 16 ounces))
                 (mix
                     (mix
                          (quote (flour 2 cups))
                          (quote (oatmeal 2 cups))
                          (quote (salt .5 teaspoon))
                          (quote (baking-powder 1 teaspoon))
                          (quote (baking-soda 1 teaspoon)))
                     (mix
                          (quote (eggs 2 large))
                          (quote (vanilla 1 teaspoon))
                          (cream
                               (quote (butter 1 cup))
                               (quote (sugar 2 cups)))))))))
```

Exercises

For these exercises,

$aexp1$ is $(1 + (3 \times 4))$
$aexp2$ is $((3 \uparrow 4) + 5)$
$aexp3$ is $(3 \times (4 \times (5 \times 6)))$
$aexp4$ is 5
$l1$ is ( )
$l2$ is $(3 + (66\ 6))$
$lexp1$ is (AND (OR x y) y)
$lexp2$ is (AND (NOT y) (OR u v))
$lexp3$ is (OR x y)
$lexp4$ is z

7.1 So far we have neglected functions that build representations for arithmetic expressions. For example, mk+exp

```
(define mk+exp
  (lambda (aexp1 aexp2)
    (cons aexp1
      (cons (quote +)
        (cons aexp2 ( ))))))
```

makes an arithmetic expression of the form $(aexp1 + aexp2)$, where $aexp1$, $aexp2$ are already arithmetic expressions. Write the corresponding functions mk×exp and mk↑exp.

The arithmetic expression $(1 + 3)$ can now be built by (mk+exp x y), where x is 1 and y is 3. Show how to build $aexp1$, $aexp2$, and $aexp3$.

7.2   A useful function is aexp? that checks whether an S-expression is the representation of an arithmetic expression. Write the function aexp? and test it with some of the arithmetic expressions from the chapter. Also test it with S-expressions that are not arithmetic expressions.

Example: (aexp? *aexp1*) is true,
       (aexp? *aexp2*) is true,
        (aexp? *l1*) is false,
        (aexp? *l2*) is false.

7.3   Write the function count-op that counts the operators in an arithmetic expression.

Example: (count-op *aexp1*) is 2,
       (count-op *aexp3*) is 3,
       (count-op *aexp4*) is 0.

Also write the functions count+, count×, and count↑ that count the respective operators.

Example: (count+ *aexp1*) is 1,
       (count× *aexp1*) is 1,
      (count↑ *aexp1*) is 0.

7.4   Write the function count-numbers that counts the numbers in an arithmetic expression.

Example: (count-numbers *aexp1*) is 3,
       (count-numbers *aexp3*) is 4,
       (count-numbers *aexp4*) is 1.

7.5   Since it is inconvenient to write $(3 \times (4 \times (5 \times 6)))$ for multiplying 4 numbers, we now introduce prefix notation and allow + and × expressions to contain 2, 3, or 4 subexpressions. For example, $(+ \ 3 \ 2 \ (\times \ 7 \ 8))$, $(\times \ 3 \ 4 \ 5 \ 6)$ etc. are now legal representations. ↑-expressions are also in prefix form but are still binary.

Rewrite the functions numbered? and value for the new definition of aexp.

Hint: You will need functions for extracting the third and the fourth subexpression of an arithmetic expression. You will also need a function cnt-aexp that counts the number of arithmetic subexpressions in the *list* following an operator.

Example: When *aexp1* is $(+ \ 3 \ 2 \ (\times \ 7 \ 8))$,
           aexp2 is $(\times \ 3 \ 4 \ 5 \ 6)$, and
           aexp3 is $(\uparrow \ aexp1 \ aexp2)$, then
  (cnt-aexp *aexp1*) is 3,
  (cnt-aexp *aexp2*) is 4,
  (cnt-aexp *aexp3*) is 2.

For exercises 7.6 through 7.10 we define a representation for L-expressions. An L-expression is defined in the following way: It is either:

    —(AND *l1 l2*), or
    —(OR *l1 l2*), or
    —(NOT *l*), or
    —an arbitrary symbol. We call such a symbol a *variable*.

In this definition, AND, OR, and NOT are literal atoms; *l, l1, l2* stand for arbitrary L-expressions.

7.6 Write the function lexp? that tests whether an S-expression is a representation of an L-expression.

Example: (lexp? *lexp1*) is true,
(lexp? *lexp2*) is true,
(lexp? *lexp3*) is true,
(lexp? *aexp1*) is false,
(lexp? *l2*) is false.

7.7 Write the function covered? of *lexp* and *lat* that tests whether all the variables in *lexp* are in *lat*.

Example: When *l1* is (x y z u), then
(covered? *lexp1 l1*) is true,
(covered? *lexp2 l1*) is false,
(covered? *lexp4 l1*) is true.

7.8 For the evaluation of L-expressions we will need an *alist*. An alist for L-expressions is a list of pairs. The first component of a pair is always an atom, the second one is either the number 0 (signifying false) or 1 (signifying true). The second component is referred to as the value of the variable. Write the function lookup of *var* and *alist* that returns the value of the first pair in alist whose car is eq? to *var*.

Example: When *l1* is ((x 1) (y 0)),
l2 is ((u 1) (v 1)),
l3 is ( ),
a is y,
b is u, then
(lookup *a l1*) is 0,
(lookup *b l2*) is 1,
(lookup *a l3*) has no answer.

7.9 If the list of atoms in an alist for L-expressions contains all the variables of an L-expression *lexp*, then *lexp* can be evaluated with respect to this alist. (Use the function covered? from Exercise 7.7 for the appropriate test) Write the function Mlexp of *lexp* and *alist*.

(Mlexp *lexp alist*) is true

— if *lexp* is a variable and its value is true, or

— if *lexp* is an AND-expression and both subexpressions yield true, or

— if *lexp* is an OR-expression and one of the subexpressions yields true, or

— if *lexp* is a NOT-expression and the subexpression yields false.

Otherwise Mlexp yields false. Mlexp has no answer if the expression is not covered by (firsts *alist*).

Example: When *l1* is ((x 1) (y 0) (z 0)),
l2 is ((y 0) (u 0) (v 1)), then

(Mlexp *lexp1 l1*) is false,

(Mlexp *lexp2 l2*) is true,

(Mlexp *lexp4 l1*) is false.

Hint: You will need the function lookup from Exercise 7.8.

7.10 Extend the representation of L-expressions to AND and OR expressions that contain several subexpressions, i.e.,

(AND x (OR u v w) y).

Rewrite the function Mlexp from Exercise 7.9 for this representation.

Hint: Exercise 7.5 is a similar extension of arithmetic expressions.

Chapter 8

Friends and Relations

Is this a *set*? (apple peaches apple plum)	No, since apple appears more than once.

(set? *lat*), where *lat* is (apples peaches pears plums)	*t*, because no atom appears more than once.

(set? *lat*), where *lat* is ( )	*t*, because no atom appears more than once.

Try to write set?

```
(define set?
  (lambda (lat)
    (cond
      ((null? lat) t)
      (t (cond
            ((member? (car lat) (cdr lat))
             nil)
            (t (set? (cdr lat)))))))))
```

Simplify set?

```
(define set?
  (lambda (lat)
    (cond
      ((null? lat) t)
      ((member? (car lat) (cdr lat)) nil)
      (t (set? (cdr lat))))))
```

Does this work for the example (apple 3 pear 4 9 apple 3 4)	Yes, since member? is now written using equal? instead of eq?

Were you surprised to see the function member? appear in the definition of set?	You should not be, because we have written member? already, and now we can use it whenever we like.

What is (makeset *lat*), where
    lat is (apple peach pear peach
        plum apple lemon peach)
	(apple peach pear plum lemon).

Try to write makeset, using member?	**(define** makeset
	    (lambda (*lat*)
	        (cond
	            ((null? *lat*) **(quote** ( )))
	            ((member? (car *lat*) (cdr *lat*))
	             (makeset (cdr *lat*)))
	            (t (cons (car *lat*)
	                 (makeset (cdr *lat*)))))))))

Are you surprised to see how short this is?	We hope so. But don't be afraid. It's right.

Using the definition that you just wrote,
what is the result of (makeset *lat*), where
    lat is (apple peach pear peach
        plum apple lemon peach)
	(pear plum apple lemon peach).

Try to write makeset, using multirember.	**(define** makeset
	    (lambda (*lat*)
	        (cond
	            ((null? *lat*) **(quote** ( )))
	            (t (cons (car *lat*)
	                 (makeset
	                     (multirember
	                         (car *lat*) (cdr *lat*)))))))))

What is the result of (makeset *lat*) using this
second definition, where
    lat is (apple peach pear peach
        plum apple lemon peach)
	(apple peach pear plum lemon).

Can you describe in your own words how the second definition of makeset works?

Here are our words:
"Makeset saves the first atom in the lat, and then recurs, after removing all occurrences of the first atom from the rest of the lat."

Does the second makeset work for the example

    (apple 3 pear 4 9 apple 3 4)

Yes, since multirember is now written using equal? instead of eq?

What is (subset? *set1* *set2*), where
  set1 is (5 chicken wings), and
  set2 is (5 hamburgers
        2 pieces fried chicken and
        light duckling wings)

t, because each atom in *set1* is also in *set2*.

What is (subset? *set1* *set2*), where
  set1 is (4 pounds of horseradish), and
  set2 is (four pounds chicken and
        5 ounces horseradish)

nil.

Try to write subset?

```
(define subset?
  (lambda (set1 set2)
    (cond
      ((null? set1) t)
      (t (cond
           ((member? (car set1) set2)
            (subset? (cdr set1) set2))
           (t nil))))))
```

Try to write a shorter version of subset?

```
(define subset?
  (lambda (set1 set2)
    (cond
      ((null? set1) t)
      ((member? (car set1) set2)
       (subset? (cdr set1) set2))
      (t nil))))
```

Try to write subset? with (and ...).

```
(define subset?
  (lambda (set1 set2)
    (cond
      ((null? set1) t)
      (t (and
           (member? (car set1) set2)
           (subset? (cdr set1) set2))))))
```

What is (eqset? set1 set2), where
    set1 is (6 large chickens with wings), and
    set2 is (6 chickens with large wings)

t.

Try to write eqset?

```
(define eqset?
  (lambda (set1 set2)
    (cond
      ((subset? set1 set2)
       (subset? set2 set1))
      (t nil))))
```

Can you write eqset? with only one cond-line?

```
(define eqset?
  (lambda (set1 set2)
    (cond
      (t (and
           (subset? set1 set2)
           (subset? set2 set1))))))
```

Write the one-liner.

```
(define eqset?
  (lambda (set1 set2)
    (and
      (subset? set1 set2)
      (subset? set2 set1))))
```

(intersect? *set1 set2*), where
  set1 is (tomatoes and macaroni), and
  set2 is (macaroni and cheese)

t,
  because at least one atom in *set1* is in
  set2.

Try to write intersect?

```
(define intersect?
  (lambda (set1 set2)
    (cond
      ((null? set1) nil)
      (t (cond
           ((member? (car set1) set2) t)
           (t (intersect?
                (cdr set1) set2)))))))
```

Try to write the shorter version.

```
(define intersect?
  (lambda (set1 set2)
    (cond
      ((null? set1) nil)
      ((member? (car set1) set2) t)
      (t (intersect? (cdr set1) set2)))))
```

Try writing intersect? with (**or** ...).

```
(define intersect?
  (lambda (set1 set2)
    (cond
      ((null? set1) nil)
      (t (or
           (member? (car set1) set2)
           (intersect?
             (cdr set1) set2))))))
```

Look back at subset? and compare for similarities.

What is (intersect *set1 set2*), where
  set1 is (tomatoes and macaroni), and
  set2 is (macaroni and cheese)

(and macaroni).

Try to write intersect.

```
(define intersect
  (lambda (set1 set2)
    (cond
      ((null? set1) (quote ( )))
      ((member? (car set1) set2)
       (cons (car set1)
         (intersect (cdr set1) set2)))
      (t (intersect (cdr set1) set2)))))
```

Rewrite intersect with
  (member? (car *set1*) *set2*)
replaced by
  (not (member? (car *set1*) *set2*))

```
(define intersect
  (lambda (set1 set2)
    (cond
      ((null? set1) (quote ( )))
      ((not (member? (car set1) set2))
       (intersect (cdr set1) set2))
      (t (cons (car set1)
           (intersect (cdr set1) set2))))))
```

Confused?	Write out the long versions and start simplifying when they are correct.

What is (union *set1 set2*), where
   set1 is (tomatoes and macaroni casserole),
and
   set2 is (macaroni and cheese)
	(tomatoes casserole macaroni and cheese).

Try to write union.

```
(define union
  (lambda (set1 set2)
    (cond
      ((null? set1) set2)
      ((member? (car set1) set2)
       (union (cdr set1) set2))
      (t (cons (car set1)
               (union (cdr set1) set2))))))
```

What is this function?

```
(define xxx
  (lambda (set1 set2)
    (cond
      ((null? set1) (quote ( )))
      ((member? (car set1) set2)
       (xxx (cdr set1) set2))
      (t (cons (car set1)
               (xxx (cdr set1) set2))))))
```

In our words:
   "It is a function which returns all the
      atoms in *set1* that are not in *set2*."
That is, xxx is the complement function.

What is (intersectall *l-set*), where *l-set* is ((a b c) (c a d e) (e f g h a b))	(a).

What is (intersectall *l-set*), where
   l-set is ((6 pears and)
         (3 peaches and 6 peppers)
         (8 pears and 6 plums)
         (and 6 prunes with lots of apples))

(6 and).

Now, using whatever help functions you need, write intersectall assuming that the list of sets is non-empty.

```
(define intersectall
  (lambda (l-set)
    (cond
      ((null? (cdr l-set)) (car l-set))
      (t (intersect (car l-set)
           (intersectall (cdr l-set)))))))
```

Is this a *pair*?
  (pear pear)

Yes, because it is a list with only two atoms.

Is this a pair?
  (3 7)

Yes.

Is this a pair?
  (2 pair)

Yes.

Is this a pair?
  (full house)

Yes.

How can you refer to the first atom of a pair?

By taking the car of the pair.

How can you refer to the second atom of a pair?

By taking the car of the cdr of the pair.

How can you make a pair with two atoms?

You cons the first atom onto the cons of the second atom onto ( ). That is,
(cons *a1* (cons *a2* (**quote** ( )))).

```
(define first
  (lambda (p)
    (cond
      (t (car p)))))
```

```
(define second
  (lambda (p)
    (cond
      (t (car (cdr p)))))))
```

They will be used to make representations of pairs and to get hold of parts of representations of pairs.
    See Chapter 7.

They will be used to improve *readability*,
    as you will soon see.

Redefine first, second, and build as one-liners.

Does the definition of build *require* atoms as arguments?

```
(define build
  (lambda (a1 a2)
    (cond
      (t (cons a1
          (cons a2 (quote ( ))))))))
```

What possible uses do these three functions have?

Can you write third as a one-liner?

```
(define third
  (lambda (l)
    (car (cdr (cdr l)))))
```

Is *l* a *rel*, where
    l is (apples peaches pumpkin pie)

No, since *l* is not a *list* of pairs. We use rel to stand for relation.

Is *l* a rel, where
    l is ((apples peaches)
        (pumpkin pie)
        (apples peaches))

No, since *l* is not a *set* of pairs.

Is *l* a rel, where *l* is ((apples peaches) (pumpkin pie))	Yes.
Is *l* a rel, where *l* is ((4 3) (4 2) (7 6) (6 2) (3 4))	Yes.
Is *rel* a *fun*, where *rel* is ((4 3) (4 2) (7 6) (6 2) (3 4))	No. We use fun to stand for function.

What is (fun? *rel*), where
  rel is ((8 3) (4 2) (7 6) (6 2) (3 4))
	t, because (firsts *rel*) is a set
	    —See Chapter 3.

Try to write fun?

How about this?

```
(define fun?
  (lambda (rel)
    (cond
      ((null? rel) t)
      ((member*
         (first (car rel)) (cdr rel))
       nil)
      (t (fun? (cdr rel))))))
```

When will this definition of fun? work?

When
  (not (intersect? (firsts *rel*) (seconds *rel*))).

Try again to write (fun? *rel*) so it will work for the case where
  rel is ((8 3) (4 2) (7 6) (6 2) (3 4))

```
(define fun?
  (lambda (rel)
    (cond
      ((null? rel) t)
      ((member?
         (first (car rel)) (firsts (cdr rel)))
       nil)
      (t (fun? (cdr rel))))))
```

Rewrite fun? with set?

```
(define fun?
  (lambda (rel)
    (set? (firsts rel))))
```

What is (revrel rel), where
   rel is ((8 a) (pumpkin pie) (got sick))

((a 8) (pie pumpkin) (sick got)).

Try to write revrel.

```
(define revrel
  (lambda (rel)
    (cond
      ((null? rel) (quote ( )))
      (t (cons
           (build
             (second (car rel))
             (first (car rel)))
           (revrel (cdr rel)))))))
```

Would the following also be correct:

```
(define revrel
  (lambda (rel)
    (cond
      ((null? rel) (quote ( )))
      (t (cons
           (cons
             (car (cdr (car rel)))
             (cons
               (car (car rel))
               (quote ( ))))
           (revrel (cdr rel)))))))
```

Yes, but now do you see how representation aids readability?

Can you guess why *fun* is not a *fullfun*, where
   fun is ((8 3) (4 2) (7 6) (6 2) (3 4))

fun is not a fullfun, since the 2 appears more than once as a second atom of a pair.

Why is *t* the value of (fullfun? *fun*), where *fun* is ((8 3) (4 8) (7 6) (6 2) (3 4))	Because the list (3 8 6 2 4) is a set.

What is (fullfun? *fun*), where
  fun is ((grape raisin)
       (plum prune)
       (stewed prune))
	nil.

What is (fullfun? *fun*), where
  fun is ((grape raisin)
       (plum prune)
       (stewed grape))
	t, because the list (raisin prune grape) is a set.

Try to write (fullfun? *fun*)

```
(define fullfun?
  (lambda (fun)
    (set? (seconds fun))))
```

What is another function name for fullfun?	one-to-one?

Can you think of a second way to write one-to-one?

```
(define one-to-one?
  (lambda (fun)
    (fun? (revrel fun))))
```

If one of the ways you just wrote that last function was:

> 1. Sitting down
> 2. Standing up
> 3. Standing on your head

You were wrong!

Exercises

For these exercises,

$$r1 \text{ is } ((a \text{ } b) \text{ } (a \text{ } a) \text{ } (b \text{ } b))$$
$$r2 \text{ is } ((c \text{ } c))$$
$$r3 \text{ is } ((a \text{ } c) \text{ } (b \text{ } c))$$
$$r4 \text{ is } ((a \text{ } b) \text{ } (b \text{ } a))$$
$$f1 \text{ is } ((a \text{ } 1) \text{ } (b \text{ } 2) \text{ } (c \text{ } 2) \text{ } (d \text{ } 1))$$
$$f2 \text{ is } (\text{ })$$
$$f3 \text{ is } ((a \text{ } 2) \text{ } (b \text{ } 1))$$
$$f4 \text{ is } ((1 \text{ } \$) \text{ } (3 \text{ } *))$$
$$d1 \text{ is } (a \text{ } b)$$
$$d2 \text{ is } (c \text{ } d)$$
$$x \text{ is } a$$

8.1 Write the function domset of *rel* which makes a set of all the atoms in *rel*. This set is referred to as *domain of discourse* of the relation *rel*.

Example: (domset *r1*) is (a b),

   (domset *r2*) is (c),

   (domset *r3*) is (a b c).

Also write the function idrel of *s* which makes a relation of all pairs of the form (*d d*) where *d* is an atom of the set *s*. (idrel *s*) is called the *identity relation on s*.

Example: (idrel *d1*) is ((a a) (b b)),

   (idrel *d2*) is ((c c) (d d)),

   (idrel *f2*) is ( ).

8.2 Write the function reflexive? which tests whether a relation is *reflexive*. A relation is reflexive if it contains all pairs of the form (*d d*) where *d* is an element of its domain of discourse (see Exercise 8.1).

Example: (reflexive? *r1*) is true,

   (reflexive? *r2*) is true,

   (reflexive? *r3*) is false.

8.3 Write the function symmetric? which tests whether a relation is *symmetric*. A relation is symmetric if it is eqset? to its revrel.

Example: (symmetric? *r1*) is false,
 (symmetric? *r2*) is true,
 (symmetric? *f2*) is true.

Also write the function antisymmetric? which tests whether a relation is *antisymmetric*. A relation is antisymmetric if the intersection of the relation with its revrel is a subset of the identity relation on its domain of discourse (see Exercise 8.1).

Example: (antisymmetric *r1*) is true,
 (antisymmetric *r2*) is true,
 (antisymmetric *r4*) is false.

And finally, this is the function asymmetric? which tests whether a relation is asymmetric:

```
(define asymmetric?
  (lambda (rel)
    (null? (intersect rel (revrel rel)))))
```

Find out which of the sample relations is asymmetric. Characterize asymmetry in one sentence.

8.4 Write the function Fapply of f and x which returns the value of f at place x. That is, it returns the second of the pair whose first is eq? to x.

Example: (Fapply *f1 x*) is 1,
 (Fapply *f2 x*) has no answer,
 (Fapply *f3 x*) is 2.

8.5 Write the function Fcomp of f and g which composes two functions. If g contains an element (x y) and f contains an element (y z), then the composed function (Fcomp f g) will contain (x z).

Example: (Fcomp *f1 f4*) is ( ),
 (Fcomp *f1 f3*) is ( ),
 (Fcomp *f4 f1*) is ((a $) (d $)),
 (Fcomp *f4 f3*) is ((b $)).

Hint: The function Fapply from Exercise 8.4 may be useful.

8.6 Write the function Rapply of *rel* and x which returns the *value set* of *rel* at place x. The value set is the set of second components of all the pairs whose first component is eq? to x.

Example: (Rapply *f1 x*) is (1),
 (Rapply *r1 x*) is (b a),
 (Rapply *f2 x*) is ( ).

8.7 Write the function Rin of x and *set* which produces a relation of pairs $(x\ d)$ where d is an element of *set*.

Example: (Rin x $d1$) is ((a a) (a b)),

(Rin x $d2$) is ((a c) (a d)),

(Rin x $f2$) is ( ).

8.8 Relations can be composed with the following function:

```
(define Rcomp
  (lambda (rel1 rel2)
    (cond
      ((null? rel1) (quote ( )))
      (t (union
           (Rin
             (first (car rel1))
             (Rapply rel2 (second (car rel1))))
           (Rcomp (cdr rel1) rel2))))))
```

See Exercises 8.6 and 8.7.

Find the values of (Rcomp $r1$ $r3$), (Rcomp $r1$ $f1$), and (Rcomp $r1$ $r1$).

8.9 Write the function transitive? which tests whether a relation is transitive. A relation *rel* is *transitive* if the composition of *rel* with *rel* is a subset of *rel* (see Exercise 8.8).

Example: (transitive? $r1$) is true,

(transitive? $r3$) is true,

(transitive? $f1$) is true.

Find a relation for which transitive? yields false.

8.10 Write the functions quasi-order?, partial-order?, and equivalence? which test whether a relation is a *quasi-order*, a *partial-order*, or an *equivalence relation*, respectively. A relation is a

—quasi-order if it is reflexive and transitive,

—partial-order if it is a quasi-order and antisymmetric,

—equivalence relation if it is a quasi-order and symmetric.

See Exercises 8.2, 8.3, and 8.9.

Chapter 9

Lambda The Ultimate

Remember what we did in rember and insertL at the end of Chapter 6?	We replaced eq? by equal?
Can you write a function rember-f that would use either eq? or equal?	No, because we have not yet told you how to do this.
How can you make rember remove the first a from (b c a)	By passing a and (b c a) as arguments to rember.
How can you make rember remove the first c from (b c a)	By passing c and (b c a) as arguments to rember.
How can you make rember-f use equal? instead of eq?	By passing equal? as an argument to rember-f.

What is (rember-f *test?* *a* *l*), where
   test? is =,[1]
   a is 5, and
   l is (6 2 5 3)
	(6 2 3).

[1] L: `(setq = (function =))` or `(setq = #'=)`.
Now try `(rember-f = 5 '(6 2 5 3))`.

What is (rember-f *test?* *a* *l*), where
   test? is eq?,[1]
   a is jelly, and
   l is (jelly beans are good)
	(beans are good).

[1] L: `(setq eq (function eq))`.

And what is (rember-f *test? a l*), where
  test? is equal?,
  a is (pop corn), and
  l is (lemonade (pop corn) and (cake))

(lemonade and (cake)).

Try to write rember-f.

```
(define rember-f
  (lambda (test? a l)
    (cond
      ((null? l) (quote ( )))
      (t (cond
           ((test? (car l) a)¹ (cdr l))
           (t (cons (car l)
                (rember-f
                  test? a (cdr l)))))))))
```

This is good!

---

¹ L: (funcall test? (car l) a). Use funcall when
invoking a function argument.

What about the short version?

```
(define rember-f
  (lambda (test? a l)
    (cond
      ((null? l) (quote ( )))
      ((test? (car l) a) (cdr l))
      (t (cons (car l)
           (rember-f test? a (cdr l)))))))
```

How does (rember-f *test? a l*) act where
test? is eq?

(rember-f *test? a l*), where *test?* is eq?, acts
like rember.

And what about (rember-f *test? a l*) where
test? is always equal?

This is just rember with eq? replaced by
equal?

Now we have four functions which do *almost* the same thing.	Yes:
	  rember with =,
	  rember with equal?,
	  rember with eq?, and
	  rember-f.

And rember-f can simulate all the others.	Yes, so let's *generate* all the other versions with rember-f.
What kind of values can functions return?	Lists, symbols, numbers, *t*, and *nil*.
What about functions themselves?	Yes, but you probably did not know that yet.
Can you say what (**lambda** (*a l*) ...) does?	(**lambda** (*a l*) ...) indicates that the expression is a function that takes two arguments, *a* and *l*.

Now what is
  (**lambda** (*a*)
    (**lambda** (*x*)
      (eq? *x a*)))
	It is a function that, when passed an argument *a* returns the function
	  (**lambda** (*x*)
	    (eq? *x a*))
	where *a* is just that argument.

Using (**define** ...), give the preceding function a name.	
	(**define** eq?-c
	  (**lambda** (*a*)
	    (**lambda** (*x*)
	      (eq? *x a*))))[1]
	
	This is our choice.

---

[1]   L: (defun eq?-c (a)
      (function
        (lambda (x)
          (eq x a))))

What is (eq?-c k), where
   k is salad

Its value is a function that takes x as an argument and tests whether it is eq? to salad.

So let's give it a name using (**define** ...):

> (**define**[1] eq?-salad (eq?-c k))

where k is salad.

Okay.

---

[1] L: (setq eq?-salad (eq?-c 'salad)).
Use setq to define a function that will be funcall*ed*.

(eq?-salad y), where y is tuna

nil.

(eq?-salad y), where y is salad

t.

Do we need to give a name to eq?-salad

No, we may just as well ask
   ((eq?-c x) y),
where
   x is salad, and
   y is tuna.

Now you can write a function rember-f that, when passed a function as an argument, returns a function that acts like rember-f where *test?* is just that argument.

```
(define rember-f
  (lambda (test?)
    (lambda (a l)
      (cond
        ((null? l) (quote ( )))
        ((test? (car l) a) (cdr l))
        (t (cons (car l) _____ ))))))
```

is again a good try.

Describe in your own words the result of
  (rember-f *test?*),
where
  test? is eq?

A function that takes two arguments, *a* and *l*. It compares the elements of the list with *a*, and the first one that is eq? to *a* is removed.

Give a name to the function which is returned by
  (rember-f *test?*),
where
  test? is eq?

(**define** rember-eq? (rember-f *test?*))

where
  test? is eq?

What is (rember-eq? *a l*), where
  a is tuna, and
  l is (tuna salad is good)

(salad is good).

Did we need to give a name (by defining rember-eq?) to (rember-f *test?*) where
  test? is eq?

No, we could have written
  ((rember-f *test?*) *a l*)[1],
where
  test? is eq?,
  a is tuna, and
  l is (tuna salad is good).

---

[1] L: (funcall (rember-f eq)
         'tuna
         '(tuna salad is good))

Now, complete the line
  (cons (car *l*) _____)
in rember-f so that rember-f really works.

```
(define rember-f
  (lambda (test?)
    (lambda (a l)
      (cond
        ((null? l) (quote ( )))
        ((test? (car l) a) (cdr l))
        (t (cons (car l)
             ((rember-f test?)
               a (cdr l)))))))))
```

What is ((rember-f eq?) *a l*), where

    a is tuna, and

    l is (shrimp salad and tuna salad)

(shrimp salad and salad).

And now transform insertL to insertL-f the same way we have transformed rember into rember-f.

```
(define insertL-f
  (lambda (test?)
    (lambda (new old l)
      (cond
        ((null? l) (quote ( )))
        ((test? (car l) old)
         (cons new (cons old (cdr l))))
        (t (cons (car l)
             ((insertL-f test?)
               new old (cdr l))))))))
```

And, just for the exercise, do it to insertR.

```
(define insertR-f
  (lambda (test?)
    (lambda (new old l)
      (cond
        ((null? l) (quote ( )))
        ((test? (car l) old)
         (cons old (cons new (cdr l))))
        (t (cons (car l)
             ((insertR-f test?)
               new old (cdr l))))))))
```

---

insertR and insertL are very similar.

Yes, only the middle piece is a little bit different.

Can you write a function insert-g which would insert either at the left or at the right?

If you can, get yourself some coffee cake and relax! Otherwise, don't give up. You'll see it in a minute.

Which pieces differ?	The second lines differ from each other. In insertL it is:
	((eq? (car *l*) *old*) (cons *new* (cons *old* (cdr *l*))))),
	but in insertR it is:
	((eq? (car *l*) *old*) (cons *old* (cons *new* (cdr *l*))))).

Put the difference in words!	We say: "The two functions cons *old* and *new* in a different order onto the cdr of the list *l*."

So how can we get rid of the difference?	You probably guessed it: by passing in a function which expresses the appropriate cons*ing*.

Define a function seqL which
 1. takes three arguments, and
 2. cons*es* the first argument onto the result of cons*ing* the second argument onto the third argument.
	``
	(define seqL
	  (lambda (new old l)
	    (cons new (cons old l))))
	``

What is:
 ``
(define seqR
  (lambda (new old l)
    (cons old (cons new l))))
``
	A function which
	 1. takes three arguments, and
	 2. cons*es* the second argument onto the result of cons*ing* the first argument onto the third argument.

Do you know why we wrote these functions?	Because they express what the two differing lines in insertL and insertR express.

Try to write the function insert-g of one
argument *seq*,
   which is insertL,
when *seq* is seqL, and
   which is insertR,
when *seq* is seqR.

```
(define insert-g
  (lambda (seq)
    (lambda (new old l)
      (cond
        ((null? l) (quote ( )))
        ((eq? (car l) old)
         (seq new old (cdr l)))
        (t (cons (car l)
             ((insert-g seq)
               new old (cdr l))))))))
```

Now define insertL with insert-g.

```
(define insertL (insert-g seqL))
```

And insertR.

```
(define insertR (insert-g seqR))
```

Is there something unusual about these two
definitions?

Yes. Earlier we would probably have written
   (**define** insertL (insert-g *seq*)),
where
  seq is seqL,
and
   (**define** insertR (insert-g *seq*)),
where
  seq is seqR.
But when you pass functions as arguments
this is not necessary.

Was it necessary to give names to seqL and
seqR

Not really. We could have passed their definitions instead.

Define insertL again with insert-g. Do not
pass in seqL this time.

```
(define insertL
  (insert-g
    (lambda (new old l)
      (cons new (cons old l)))))
```

Is this better?	Yes, because you do not need to remember as many names. You can (rember *func-name* "your-mind"), where *func-name* is seqL.

Do you remember the definition of subst	Here is the definition of subst.

```
(define subst
  (lambda (new old l)
    (cond
      ((null? l) (quote ( )))
      ((eq? (car l) old)
       (cons new (cdr l)))
      (t (cons (car l)
          (subst new old (cdr l)))))))
```

Does this look familiar?	Yes, it looks like insertL or insertR. Just the answer of the second cond-line is different.

Define a function like seqL or seqR for subst.	What do you think about

```
(define seqS
  (lambda (new old l)
    (cons new l)))
```

| And now define subst using insert-g. | ```
(define subst (insert-g seqS))
``` |

And what do you think xxx is	Surprise: It is our old friend rember!

```
(define xxx
  (lambda (a l)
    ((insert-g seqrem) nil a l)))
```

where

```
(define seqrem
  (lambda (new old l)
    l))
```

Hint: Step through the evaluation of
    (xxx *a l*),
where
    a is sausage, and
    l is (pizza with sausage and bacon).
What is the role of nil?
```

What you have just seen is the power of abstraction.

The Tenth Commandment

Abstract functions with common structures into a single function.

Have we seen similar functions before?	Yes, we have even seen functions with similar lines.

Do you remember value from Chapter 7?

```
(define value
  (lambda (aexp)
    (cond
      ((number? aexp) aexp)
      ((eq? (operator aexp)
            (quote plus))
       (+ (value (1st-sub-exp aexp))
          (value (2nd-sub-exp aexp))))
      ((eq? (operator aexp)
            (quote times))
       (× (value (1st-sub-exp aexp))
          (value (2nd-sub-exp aexp))))
      (t (↑ (value (1st-sub-exp aexp))
            (value (2nd-sub-exp aexp)))))))
```

Do you see the similarities?	The last three lines are the same except for the +, ×, and ↑.

Can you write a function atom-to-function that:
1. Takes one argument, *x*, and
2. Returns the function +
     if (eq? *x* (quote +)),
   Returns the function ×
     if (eq? *x* (quote ×)), and
   Returns the function ↑
     if (eq? *x* (quote ↑))

```
(define atom-to-function
  (lambda (x)
    (cond
      ((eq? x (quote +)) + )
      ((eq? x (quote ×)) × )
      ((eq? x (quote ↑)) ↑ ))))
```

What is (atom-to-function (operator *aexp*)), where

   aexp is (+ 5 3)

The function +, not the symbol +.

Can you use atom-to-function to rewrite value with only two lines inside the (**cond** ...).

Of course.

```
(define value
  (lambda (aexp)
    (cond
      ((number? aexp) aexp)
      (t ((atom-to-function
            (operator aexp))
          (value (1st-sub-exp aexp))
          (value (2nd-sub-exp aexp)))))))
```

Is this quite a bit shorter than the first version?

Yes, but that's okay. We haven't changed its meaning.

Write the functions subset? and intersect? next to each other.

```
(define subset?
  (lambda (set1 set2)
    (cond
      ((null? set1) t)
      (t (and
           (member? (car set1) set2)
           (subset? (cdr set1) set2))))))
```

and

```
(define intersect?
  (lambda (set1 set2)
    (cond
      ((null? set1) nil)
      (t (or
           (member? (car set1) set2)
           (intersect?
             (cdr set1) set2))))))
```

Again, these functions have the same structure.	Yes, they only differ in (**and** ...) and (**or** ...), t and nil, and the name of the recursive function.

So let's abstract them into a function
   (set-f? *logical? const*)
which can generate subset? and intersect?
	``
	(define set-f?
	  (lambda (logical? const)
	    (lambda (set1 set2)
	      (cond
	        ((null? set1) const)
	        (t (logical?
	             (member? (car set1) set2)
	             ((set-f? logical? const)
	               (cdr set1) set2)))))))
	``

Now, define subset? and intersect? using the function set-f?	`(define subset? (set-f? and t))`
	`(define intersect? (set-f? or nil))`
	almost work.

Why don't they?	Because **and** and **or** are not really functions. They cannot be passed as arguments.

So we write functions that do act like
(**and** ...) and (**or** ...).
	Here they are:
	
	``
	(define and-prime
	  (lambda (x y)
	    (and x y)))
	``
	
	``
	(define or-prime
	  (lambda (x y)
	    (or x y)))
	``
	
	And we can pass them to set-f?

What does
  (**and** nil (subset? x y))
do, where
  x is (red wine tastes good), and
  y is (it goes well with brie cheese)
	It returns *nil without* ever asking the second question!

What does
  (or-prime t (intersect? x y))
do, where
  x is (red wine tastes good), and
  y is (it goes well with brie cheese)
	It evaluates *both* questions. The first one to *t*, the second one to *nil*, and then it returns *t*.

What would (**or** ...) have done instead?	It would have answered *t without* asking the second question.
Why are both (**and** ...) and (**or** ...) unusual?	They do not always ask the second question.[1]

---

[1] Because of this property, neither (**and** ...) nor (**or** ...) can be **defined** as functions in terms of (**cond** ...), but both (**and** ...) and (**or** ...) can be *expressed* in terms of (**cond** ...):

$$(\textbf{and } \alpha \ \beta) = (\textbf{cond } (\alpha \ \beta) \ (\text{t nil}))$$

and

$$(\textbf{or } \alpha \ \beta) \ = (\textbf{cond } (\alpha \ \text{t}) \ (\text{t } \beta))$$

Macros are a mechanism for expressing these relationships.

Which values do we need to ask the question
  (**or** x (intersect? (cdr *set1*) *set2*)),
where x is the result of
  (member? (car *set1*) *set2*)
	Only *set1* and *set2*. The rest can be reconstructed.

Now write
   or-prime for intersect?,
and
   and-prime for subset?

```
(define or-prime
  (lambda (x set1 set2)
    (or x (intersect? (cdr set1) set2))))
```

```
(define and-prime
  (lambda (x set1 set2)
    (and x (subset? (cdr set1) set2))))
```

Rewrite set-f? so that it can generate sub-set? and intersect? with and-prime and or-prime.

```
(define set-f?
  (lambda (logical? const)
    (lambda (set1 set2)
      (cond
        ((null? set1) const)
        (t (logical?
              (member? (car set1) set2)
              set1
              set2))))))
```

But we have not yet defined intersect? and subset?

Well, that's what we defined or-prime and and-prime for.

Do it!

```
(define intersect? (set-f? or-prime nil))
```

```
(define subset? (set-f? and-prime t))
```

Didn't we need intersect? for or-prime

No, we only assumed we could define it. And now we have it.

That sounds awfully ...

Recursive.

So what is recursion?

Hold tight, take a deep breath, and plunge forward when you're ready.

Recall the definition of multirember. Simplify multirember by removing the inner (**cond** ...).

```
(define multirember
  (lambda (a l)
    (cond
      ((null? l) (quote ( )))
      ((eq? (car l) a)
       (multirember a (cdr l)))
      (t (cons (car l)
               (multirember a (cdr l)))))))
```

What is
   (multirember (**quote** curry) *l*)
where
   l is (a b c curry e curry g curry)

This is an application where *l* is associated with the value
   (a b c curry e curry g curry).
It has the value
   (a b c e g).

If we wrap this application by
   (**lambda** (*l*) ...)
what do we create?

We create a function
   (**lambda** (*l*)
      (multirember (**quote** curry) *l*)).

We define the new function, and give it a name.

(a b c e g).

```
(define Mrember-curry
  (lambda (l)
    (multirember (quote curry) l)))
```

What is
   (Mrember-curry
      (**quote** (a b c curry e curry g curry)))

Rewrite Mrember-curry using three questions.

```
(define Mrember-curry
  (lambda (l)
    (cond
      ((null? l) (quote ( )))
      ((eq? (car l) (quote curry))
       (Mrember-curry (cdr l)))
      (t (cons (car l)
           (Mrember-curry (cdr l)))))))
```

Compare curry-maker to insert-g.

```
(define curry-maker
  (lambda (future)
    (lambda (l)
      (cond
        ((null? l) (quote ( )))
        ((eq? (car l) (quote curry))
         ((curry-maker future) (cdr l)))
        (t (cons (car l)
             ((curry-maker future)
              (cdr l))))))))
```

The function curry-maker is like the function Mrember-curry in the same way that insert-g is like insertL. It takes one extra argument *future*. When it is applied to an argument, it returns a function that looks like Mrember-curry except for the applications (curry-maker *future*).

Does curry-maker ever use the argument *future*

No, unlike *seq*, *future* is just passed around. When curry-maker reaches the end of the list, *future* is not used.

Can curry-maker then make Mrember-curry

Yes, it can.

Define Mrember-curry using curry-maker.

```
(define Mrember-curry (curry-maker 0))
```

Does it matter what we use to define Mrember-curry

No, *future* is never used.

Can we use curry-maker to define Mrember-curry with curry-maker	Of course, (**define** Mrember-curry (curry-maker curry-maker))
If we define Mrember-curry this way what does *future* become?	The value of *future* is curry-maker.
But can't we then just use *future* to replace curry-maker in curry-maker	Yes, we sure can.

We call the function we just described "function-maker" because its results are functions. Write function-maker.	(**define** function-maker
	  (**lambda** (*future*)
	    (**lambda** (*l*)
	      (**cond**
	        ((null? *l*) (**quote** ( )))
	        ((eq? (car *l*) (**quote** curry))
	        ((*future future*) (cdr *l*)))
	        (t (cons (car *l*)
	          ((*future future*) (cdr *l*)))))))))

Describe in your own words the function function-maker.	Here is what we say: "When the function function-maker is applied to one argument that is a function and that returns Mrember-curry when applied to one argument, then function-maker yields Mrember-curry."
That explanation sounds as if function-maker needs an argument that is just like function-maker in order to construct Mrember-curry.	Yes, that is exactly what it says.

Write Mrember-curry using just
function-maker.

> (**define** Mrember-curry
>   (function-maker _____))

> (**define** Mrember-curry
>   (function-maker function-maker))

Try studying the function with
   (a b c curry e curry g h curry i).

If we define Mrember-curry this way what
does *future* become?

The value of *future* is function-maker.

Why does this definition of Mrember-curry
work?

Because the value of (*future future*) is the
same as (function-maker function-maker)
which is the same as Mrember-curry.

Do we have to define (or give a name to)
function-maker?

No, because function-maker does not appear
within its definition.

Do we have to associate a name with
Mrember-curry using (**define** ...)

No, because Mrember-curry does not appear
within its definition.

True or false: *no* recursive function needs to
be given a name with (**define** ...)

True. We chose Mrember-curry as an arbitrary recursive function.

True or false: instances of add1 can be replaced by
   (**lambda** (*x*) (add1 *x*))

True, because
   ((**lambda** (*x*) (add1 *x*)) *n*)
is
   $n + 1$.

True or false: instances of
   (**lambda** (*x*) (add1 *x*))
can be replaced by
   (**lambda** (*y*)
      ((**lambda** (*x*) (add1 *x*)) *y*))

True, because adding the extra wrapping has
no effect.

True or false: instances of
  (lambda (x) (add1 x)**)**
can be replaced by
  (lambda (x)
    ((lambda (x) (add1 x)**)** x)**)**

True, because in general for any function f of one argument, f can be replaced by
  (lambda (x) (f x)**)**.
Can you think of an f where this is false?

Is the definition below the same as the function-maker we defined earlier?

```
(define function-maker
  (lambda (future)
    (lambda (l)
      (cond
        ((null? l) (quote ( )))
        ((eq? (car l) (quote curry))
         (
           (lambda (arg)
             ((future future) arg))

           (cdr l)))
        (t (cons (car l)
           (
             (lambda (arg)
               ((future future) arg))

             (cdr l))))))))
```

Yes, because for an arbitrary function f we can always replace it by
  (lambda (x) (f x)**)**.
In our case f is the expression
  (*future future*),
and
  x is *arg*.

Is the definition below the same as the function-maker we just defined?

```
(define function-maker
  (lambda (future)
    ((lambda (recfun)
       (lambda (l)
         (cond
           ((null? l) (quote ( )))
           ((eq? (car l)
                 (quote curry))
            (recfun (cdr l)))
           (t (cons (car l)
                    (recfun (cdr l)))))))
     (lambda (arg)
       ((future future) arg)))))
```

Yes, because the atom *l* does not appear in
  (**lambda** (*arg*)
    ((*future future*) *arg*))
Hence, we can abstract out this piece, replacing it by an atom that is associated with it. We chose the atom *recfun*.

Can you make the definition of function-maker simpler by breaking it up into two functions?

Hint: look at the inner box.

```
(define function-maker
  (lambda (future)
    (M (lambda (arg)
         ((future future) arg)))))
```

```
(define M
  (lambda (recfun)
    (lambda (l)
      (cond
        ((null? l) (quote ( )))
        ((eq? (car l) (quote curry))
         (recfun (cdr l)))
        (t (cons (car l)
                 (recfun (cdr l))))))))
```

Why may we do this?

Because it is safe to name the expression
  (**lambda** (*recfun*) ...).

Why is it safe to name (**lambda** (*recfun*) ...)	Because all the variables are explicit arguments to M, or they are primitives.

Write Mrember-curry without using function-maker.

  Hint: Use the most recent definition of function-maker in two different places.

From

```
(define Mrember-curry
   (function-maker function-maker))
```

we get

```
(define Mrember-curry
   ((lambda (future)
      (M (lambda (arg)
            ((future future) arg))))
    (lambda (future)
      (M (lambda (arg)
            ((future future) arg))))))
```

Do you need a rest?	Yes? Then take one.

Abstract the definition of Mrember-curry by abstracting away the association with M.

  Hint: wrap a (**lambda** (*M*) ...) around the definition.

We call this function Y.

```
(define Y
   (lambda (M)
      ((lambda (future)
         (M (lambda (arg)
               ((future future) arg))))
       (lambda (future)
         (M (lambda (arg)
               ((future future) arg)))))))
```

Write Mrember-curry using Y and M.

```
(define Mrember-curry (Y M))
```

You have just worked through the derivation of a function called "the applicative-order Y-combinator." The interesting aspect of Y is that it produces recursive definitions without the bother of requiring that the functions be named with (**define** ...). Define L so that length is

> (**define** length (Y L))

> (**define** L
>   (**lambda** (*recfun*)
>   (**lambda** (*l*)
>   (**cond**
>   ((null? *l*) 0)
>   (t (add1 (*recfun* (cdr *l*))))))))

Describe in your own words what *f* should be for (Y *f*) to work as expected.

Our words:
"*f* is a function which we want to be recursive, except that the atom *recfun* replaces the recursive call, and the whole expression is wrapped in
(**lambda** (*recfun*) ...)."

Write length using Y, but not L, by substituting the definition for L.

> (**define** length
>   (Y
>   (**lambda** (*recfun*)
>   (**lambda** (*l*)
>   (**cond**
>   ((null? *l*) 0)
>   (t (add1
>   (*recfun* (cdr *l*)))))))))

Does the Y-combinator need to be named with (**define** ...)

No.

Rewrite length without using either Y or L.

```
(define length
  ((lambda (M)
     ((lambda (future)
        (M (lambda (arg)
             ((future future) arg))))
      (lambda (future)
        (M (lambda (arg)
             ((future future) arg))))))
   (lambda (recfun)
     (lambda (l)
       (cond
         ((null? l) 0)
         (t (add1 (recfun (cdr l)))))))))
```

We observe that length does not need to be named with (**define** ...). Write an application that corresponds to

(length (**quote** (a b c)))

without using length.

```
(((lambda (M)
    ((lambda (future)
       (M (lambda (arg)
            ((future future) arg))))
     (lambda (future)
       (M (lambda (arg)
            ((future future) arg))))))
  (lambda (recfun)
    (lambda (l)
      (cond
        ((null? l) 0)
        (t (add1 (recfun (cdr l))))))))
 (quote (a b c)))
```

Whew, names may not be necessary, but they sure can be useful!

Does your hat still fit?

Perhaps not, if your mind has been stretched.

> And when your mind has returned, enjoy yourself
> with a great dinner:
>
> ((escargots garlic)
> (chicken Provençal)
> ((red wine) and Brie))
>
> is our advice.[†]

No, you don't have to eat the parentheses.

Exercises

9.1 Look up the functions firsts and seconds in Chapter 3. They can be generalized to a function map of f and l that applies f to every element in l and builds a new list with the resulting values. Write the function map. Then write the function firsts and seconds using map.

9.2 Write the function assq-sf of a, l, sk, and fk. The function searches through l which is a list of pairs until it finds a pair whose first component is eq? to a. Then the function invokes the function sk with this pair. If the search fails, $(fk\ a)$ is invoked.

Example: When a is apple,

        $b1$ is ( ),

        $b2$ is ((apple 1) (plum 2)),

        $b3$ is ((peach 3)),

        sk is (**lambda** (p)

            (build (first p) (add1 (second p)))),

        fk is (**lambda** ($name$)

           (cons

            $name$

           (**quote** (not-in-list)))), then

(assq-sf a $b1$ sk fk) is (apple not-in-list),

(assq-sf a $b2$ sk fk) is (apple 2),

(assq-sf a $b3$ sk fk) is (apple not-in-list).

9.3 In the chapter we have derived a Y-combinator that allows us to write recursive functions of one argument without using define. Here is the Y-combinator for functions of two arguments:

```
(define Y2
  (lambda (M)
    ((lambda (future)
       (M (lambda (arg1 arg2)
            ((future future) arg1 arg2))))
     (lambda (future)
       (M (lambda (arg1 arg2)
            ((future future) arg1 arg2)))))))
```

Write the functions =, rempick, and pick from Chapter 4 using Y2.

Note: There is a version of (**lambda** ...) for defining a function of an arbitrary number of arguments, and an `apply` function for applying such a function to a list of arguments. With this you can write a single Y-combinator for all functions.

9.4 With the Y-combinator we can reduce the number of arguments on which a function has to recur. For example member can be rewritten as:

```
(define member-Y
  (lambda (a l)
    ((Y (lambda (recfun)
          (lambda (l)
            (cond
              ((null? l) nil)
              (t (or
                   (eq? (car l) a)
                   (recfun (cdr l)))))))
     l)))
```

Step through the application (member-Y *a l*) where *a* is x and *l* is (y x). Rewrite the functions rember, insertR, and subst2 from Chapter 3 in a similar manner.

9.5 In Exercises 6.7 through 6.10 we saw how to use the accumulator technique. Instead of accumulators, continuation functions are sometimes used. These functions abstract what needs to be done to complete an application. For example, multisubst can be defined as:

```
(define multisubst-k
  (lambda (new old lat k)
    (cond
      ((null? lat) (k (quote ( ))))
      ((eq? (car lat) old)
       (multisubst-k new old (cdr lat)
          (lambda (d)
            (k (cons new d)))))
      (t (multisubst-k new old (cdr lat)
          (lambda (d)
            (k (cons (car lat) d))))))))
```

The initial continuation function *k* is always the function (**lambda** (x) x). Step through the application of

$$(multisubst-k \ new \ old \ lat \ k),$$

where

$$new \text{ is y,}$$
$$old \text{ is x, and}$$
$$lat \text{ is (u v x x y z x).}$$

Compare the steps to the application of multisubst to the same arguments. Write down the things you have to do when you return from a recursive application, and, next to it, write down the corresponding continuation function.

9.6 In Chapter 4 and Exercise 4.2 you wrote addvec and multvec. Abstract the two functions into a single function accum. Write the functions length and occur using accum.

9.7 In Exercise 7.3 you wrote the four functions count-op, count-+, count-×, and count-↑. Abstract them into a single function count-op-f which generates the corresponding functions if passed an appropriate help function.

9.8 Functions of no arguments are called *thunks*. If f is a thunk, it can be evaluated with (f). Consider the following version of or as a function.

```
(define or-func
  (lambda (or1 or2)
    (or (or1) (or2))))
```

Assuming that *or1* and *or2* are always thunks, convince yourself that (**or** ...) and or-func are equivalent. Consider as an example
   (**or** (null? *l*) (atom? (car *l*)))
and the corresponding application
   (or-func
      (**lambda** ( ) (null? *l*))
      (**lambda** ( ) (atom? (car *l*)))),
where
   l is ( ).
Write set-f? to take or-func and and-func. Write the functions intersect? and subset? with this set-f? function.

9.9 When you build a pair with an S-expression and a thunk (see Exercise 9.8) you get a *stream*. There are two functions defined on streams: first$ and second$.

Note: In practice, you can actually cons an S-expression directly onto a function. We prefer to stay with the less general cons function.

```
(define first$ first)
```

```
(define second$
  (lambda (str)
    ((second str))))
```

An example of a stream is (build 1 (**lambda** ( ) 2)). Let's call this stream *s*. (first$ *s*) is then 1, and (second$ *s*) is 2. Streams are interesting because they can be used to represent *unbounded* collections such as the integers. Consider the following definitions.

Str-maker is a function that takes a number n and a function *next* and produces a stream:

```
(define str-maker
  (lambda (next n)
    (build n (lambda ( ) (str-maker next (next n))))))
```

With str-maker we can now define the stream of *all* integers like this:

```
(define int (str-maker add1 0))
```

Or we can define the stream of *all* even numbers:

```
(define even (str-maker (lambda (n) (+ 2 n)) 0))
```

With the function frontier we can obtain a finite piece of a stream in a list:

```
(define frontier
  (lambda (str n)
    (cond
      ((zero? n) (quote ( )))
      (t (cons (first$ str) (frontier (second$ str) (sub1 n)))))))
```

What is (frontier int 10)? (frontier int 100)? (frontier even 23)?
Define the stream of odd numbers.

9.10 This exercise builds on the results of Exercise 9.9. Consider the following functions:

```
(define Q
  (lambda (str n)
    (cond
      ((zero? (remainder (first$ str) n))
       (Q (second$ str) n))
      (t (build (first$ str)
           (lambda ( )
             (Q (second$ str) n)))))))
```

```
(define P
  (lambda (str)
    (build (first$ str) (lambda ( ) (P (Q str (first$ str)))))))
```

They can be used to construct streams. What is the result of
                    (frontier (P (second$ (second$ int))) 10)?
What is this stream of numbers? (See Exercise 4.9 for the definition of remainder.)

Chapter 10

What is the Value
of All of This?

An entry is a pair of lists whose first list is a set. Also, the two lists must be of equal length. Make up some examples for entries.

Here are our examples:

    ((appetizer entrée beverage)
     (paté boeuf vin))

and

    ((beverage dessert)
     ((food is) (number one with us))).

How can we build an entry from a set of names and a list of values?

(**define** new-entry build)

Try to build our examples with this function.

What is (lookup-in-entry *name entry*), where
    name is entrée, and
    entry is ((appetizer entrée beverage)
            (food tastes good))

tastes.

What if *name* is dessert

In this case we would like to leave the decision about what to do with the user of lookup-in-entry.

How can we accomplish this?

lookup-in-entry will take an additional argument which is a help function that is invoked when *name* is not found in the first list of an entry.

How many arguments do you think this extra function should take?

We think it should take one, *name*. Why?

Here is our definition of lookup-in-entry.

```
(define lookup-in-entry
  (lambda (name entry entry-f)
    (lookup-in-entry-help
      name
      (first entry)
      (second entry)
      entry-f)))
```

Write the help function

```
(define lookup-in-entry-help
  (lambda (name names values entry-f)
    (cond
      ( _____  _____ )
      ( _____  _____ )
      ( _____  _____ )))))
```

```
(define lookup-in-entry-help
  (lambda (name names values entry-f)
    (cond
      ((null? names) (entry-f name))
      ((eq? (car names) name)
       (car values))
      (t (lookup-in-entry-help
           name
           (cdr names)
           (cdr values)
           entry-f)))))
```

A table (also called an *environment*) is a list of entries. Here is one example: ( ), the empty table. Make up some others.

Here is one:
```
(((appetizer entrée beverage)
  (paté boeuf vin))
 ((beverage dessert)
  ((food is) (number one with us)))).
```

The function extend-table takes an entry and a table (possibly the empty one) and creates a new table by putting the new entry in front of the old table. Define the function extend-table.

```
(define extend-table cons)
```

What is
    (lookup-in-table name table table-f)
where
    name is entrée,
    table is (((entrée dessert)
            (spaghetti spumoni))
            ((appetizer entrée beverage)
            (food tastes good))), and
    table-f is (lambda (name) ...)

It could be either spaghetti or tastes, but we will have lookup-in-table search the list of entries in order. So it is spaghetti.

Write lookup-in-table.
    Hint: don't forget to get some help.

```
(define lookup-in-table
  (lambda (name table table-f)
    (cond
      ((null? table) (table-f name))
      (t (lookup-in-entry
           name
           (car table)
           (lambda (name)
             (lookup-in-table
               name
               (cdr table)
               table-f)))))))
```

Can you describe what the following function represents:
```
(lambda (name)
  (lookup-in-table
    name
    (cdr table)
    table-f))
```

This function is the action to take when the name is not found in the first entry.

In the Preface we mentioned that sans serif font would be used to represent data. Up to this point it has hardly ever mattered. From this point on until the end of the book you must be very conscious of whether or not a particular symbol is in sans serif.

Remember to be very conscious as to whether or not a symbol is in sans serif.

Did you notice that "sans serif" was not in sans serif?

We hope so. This is "sans serif"
                                       in sans serif.

Have we chosen a good representation for programs?

Yes. They are all S-expressions so they can be data for functions.

What kind of functions?

For example, value.

What is the Value of All of This?

183

Do you remember value from Chapter 7?	Recall that value is the function that returns the natural value of expressions.
What is the value of (car (**quote** (a b c)))	a.
What is (value *e*), where *e* is (car (quote (a b c)))	a.
What is (value *e*), where *e* is (quote (car (quote (a b c))))	(car (quote (a b c))).
What is (value *e*), where *e* is (add1 6)	7
What is (value *e*) where *e* is 6	6, because numbers are self-evaluating.
What is (value *e*) where *e* is nothing	nothing has no value.

What is (value *e*) where
e is ((lambda (nothing)
    (cons nothing (quote ( ))))
  (quote
    (from nothing comes something)))
	((from nothing comes something)).

What is (value *e*) where
e is ((lambda (nothing)
    (cond
      (nothing (quote something))
      (t (quote nothing))))
  t)
	something.

What is the type of *e* where *e* is 6	*self-evaluating.
What is the type of *e* where *e* is nil	*identifier.
What is the type of *e* where *e* is cons	*identifier.
What is (value *e*) where *e* is car	(primitive car).
What is the type of *e* where *e* is nothing	*identifier.
What is the type of *e* where *e* is (lambda (x y) (cons x y))	*lambda.

What is the type of *e* where
    e is ((lambda (nothing)
          (cond
            (nothing (quote something))
            (t (quote nothing))))
      nil)
	*application.

How many types do you think there are?	We found six:
	    *self-evaluating,
	    *quote,
	    *identifier,
	    *lambda,
	    *cond, and
	    *application.

How do you think we should represent types?	We choose functions. We call these functions "actions."

If actions are functions that do "the right thing" when applied to the appropriate type of expression, what should value do?

You guessed it. It would have to find out the type of expression it was passed and then use the associated action.

Do you remember atom-to-function from Chapter 9?

We found atom-to-function useful when we rewrote value for numbered expresssions.

Below is a program that produces the correct action (or function) for each possible S-expression:

```
(define expression-to-action
  (lambda (e)
    (cond
      ((atom? e) (atom-to-action e))
      (t (list-to-action e)))))
```

Define the help function atom-to-action.[1]

```
(define atom-to-action
  (lambda (e)
    (cond
      ((number? e) *self-evaluating)
      (t *identifier))))
```

---

[1] Ill-formed S-expressions such as (quote a b) and (lambda a) are not considered here. They can be detected by an appropriate function to which S-expressions are submitted before they are passed on to the interpreter.

Now define the help function list-to-action.

```
(define list-to-action
  (lambda (e)
    (cond
      ((atom? (car e))
       (cond
         ((eq? (car e) (quote quote))
          *quote)
         ((eq? (car e) (quote lambda))
          *lambda)
         ((eq? (car e) (quote cond))
          *cond)
         (t *application)))
      (t *application))))
```

Assuming that expression-to-action works, we can use it to define value and meaning:

```
(define value
  (lambda (e)
    (meaning e (quote ( )))))
```

```
(define meaning
  (lambda (e table)
    ((expression-to-action e) e table)))
```

What is (quote ( )) in the definition of value?

It is the empty table. The function value, together with all the functions it uses, is called an *interpreter*.

How many arguments should actions take according to the above?

Two, the expression e and a table which is initially ( ).

Here is the action for self-evaluating expressions.

```
(define *self-evaluating
  (lambda (e table)
    e))
```

Is it correct?

Yes, it just returns that expression, and this is all we have to do for 0, 1, 2, ...

Here is the action for *quote.

```
(define *quote
  (lambda (e table)
    (text-of-quotation e)))
```

Define the help function text-of-quotation.

```
(define text-of-quotation second)
```

Have we used the table yet?

No, but we will in a moment.

Why do we need the table?

To remember the values of identifiers.

What is the Value of All of This?

Given that the table contains the values of identifiers, write the action *identifier.

```
(define *identifier
  (lambda (e table)
    (lookup-in-table
      e table initial-table)))
```

Here is initial-table.

```
(define initial-table
  (lambda (name)
    (cond
      ((eq? name (quote t)) t)
      ((eq? name (quote nil)) nil)
      (t (build
           (quote primitive)
           name)))))
```

When is it used?

It handles cases that are not in *table*. We defined it so that it gives values to predetermined identifiers like t, nil, cons, zero?, etc.

What is the value of (lambda (x) x)

We don't know yet, but we know that it must be the representation of a non-primitive function.

How are non-primitive functions different from primitives?

We know what primitives do; non-primitives are defined by their arguments and their function bodies.

So when we want to use a non-primitive we need to remember its formal arguments and its function body.

At least. Fortunately this is just the cdr of a lambda-expression.

And what else do we need to remember?

We will also put in the table in case we need it later.

And how do we represent this?

In a list, of course.

Here is the action *lambda.

```
(define *lambda
  (lambda (e table)
    (build (quote non-primitive)
      (cons table (cdr e)))))
```

What is (meaning e table), where
  e is (lambda (x) (cons x y)), and
  table is (((y z) ((8) 9)))

(non-primitive
  ((((y z) ((8) 9))) (x) (cons x y))).

It is probably a good idea to define some help functions for getting back the parts in this three element list (i.e., the table, the formal arguments, and the body). Write table-of, formals-of, and body-of.

```
(define table-of first)
```

```
(define formals-of second)
```

```
(define body-of third)
```

Describe (cond ...) in your own words.

It is a special form which takes a list of cond-lines. It considers each line in turn. If the question part on the left is false, then it looks at the rest of the lines. Otherwise it proceeds to answer the right part.

Here is the function evcon which does what we just said in words:

```
(define evcon
  (lambda (lines table)
    (cond
      ((meaning
         (question-of (car lines)) table)
       (meaning
         (answer-of (car lines)) table))
      (t (evcon (cdr lines) table)))))
```

Write the help functions question-of and answer-of.

```
(define question-of first)
```

```
(define answer-of second)
```

What is the Value of All of This?

| Did we violate The First Commandment? | Yes, we have not asked (null? *lines*). |

| Now use the function evcon to write the action *cond. | |

```
(define *cond
  (lambda (e table)
    (evcon (cond-lines e) table)))
```

```
(define cond-lines cdr)
```

| Aren't these help functions useful? | Yes, they make things quite a bit more readable. But you already knew this. |

| Are you now familiar with the definition of *cond | Probably not. |

| How can you become familiar with it? | The best way is to try an example. A good one is: |

   (*cond *e* *table*),
where
   e is (cond (coffee klatsch) (t party)), and
   table is (((coffee)
               (t))
              ((klatsch party)
               (5 (6)))).

| Have we seen how the table gets used? | Yes, *lambda and *identifier use it. |

| But how do the identifiers get into the table? | In the only action we have not defined, *application. |

| How is an application represented? | An application is a list of expressions whose car position contains an expression whose value is a function. |

How does an application differ from a special form, like (**and** ...), (**or** ...), or (**cond** ...).	An application must always determine the meaning of *all* its arguments.

Before we can apply a function do we have to get the meaning of all arguments?	Yes.

Write a function evlis which takes a list of (representations of) arguments and a table, and returns a list composed of the meaning of each argument.

```
(define evlis
  (lambda (args table)
    (cond
      ((null? args) (quote ( )))
      (t (cons (meaning (car args) table)
               (evlis (cdr args) table))))))
```

What else do we need before we can determine the meaning of an application?	We need to find out what its function-of *means*.

And what then?	Then we apply the meaning of the function to the meaning of the arguments.

Here is the function *application.

```
(define *application
  (lambda (e table)
    (apply
      (meaning (function-of e) table)
      (evlis (arguments-of e) table))))
```

Is it correct?

Of course. We just have to define apply, function-of, and arguments-of correctly.

Write function-of and arguments-of.

```
(define function-of car)
```

```
(define arguments-of cdr)
```

How many different kinds of functions are there?	Two: primitives and non-primitives.

What are the two representations of functions?	(primitive *primitive-name*) and (non-primitive (*table formals body*)) The list (*table formals body*) without the non-primitive tag is called a *closure*.

Write primitive? and non-primitive?

```
(define primitive?
  (lambda (l)
    (eq?
      (first l)
      (quote primitive))))
```

```
(define non-primitive?
  (lambda (l)
    (eq?
      (first l)
      (quote non-primitive))))
```

Now we can write the function apply.

Here it is:

```
(define apply¹
  (lambda (fun vals)
    (cond
      ((primitive? fun)
       (apply-primitive
         (second fun) vals))
      ((non-primitive? fun)
       (apply-closure
         (second fun) vals)))))
```

---

1   If *fun* does not evaluate to either a primitive or a non-primitive the program is ill-formed, e.g.,
    (((**lambda** (*x*) 1) 2) 3).

This is the definition of apply-primitive.

```
(define apply-primitive
  (lambda (name vals)
    (cond
      ((eq? name (quote car))
       (car (first vals)))
      ((eq? name (quote cdr))
       (   1   (first vals)))
      ((eq? name     2    )
       (cons (first vals) (second vals)))
      ((eq? name (quote eq?))
       (   3   (first vals)    4    ))
      ((eq? name (quote atom?))
       (atom?     5    ))
      ((eq? name (quote not))
       (not (first vals)))
      ((eq? name (quote null?))
       (null? (first vals)))
      ((eq? name (quote number?))
       (number? (first vals)))
      ((eq? name (quote zero?))
       (zero? (first vals)))
      ((eq? name (quote add1))
       (add1 (first vals)))
      ((eq? name (quote sub1))
       (sub1 (first vals))))))
```

Fill in the blanks.

1. cdr[1]
2. (quote cons)
3. eq?
4. (second vals)
5. (first vals)

---

[1] In apply-primitive the interpreter could check for applications of cdr to ( ) or sub1 to 0, etc.

Is apply-closure the only function left?

Yes, and apply-closure must be the part that extends the table.

How could we find the result of (f a b), where
  f is (lambda (x y) (cons x y))
  a is 1, and
  b is (2)

That's tricky. But we know what to do to find the meaning of
  (cons x y)
where
  table is (((x y)
           (1 (2)))).

What is the Value of All of This?

Why can we do this?	Here, we don't need apply-closure.

Can you generalize the last two steps?	Applying a non-primitive function to a list of values is the same as finding the meaning of the associated closure's body with its table extended by an entry of the form (*formals values*). *formals* is the *formals* of the associated closure and *values* is the result of evlis.

Have you followed all this?	If not, here is the definition of apply-closure.

```
(define apply-closure
  (lambda (closure vals)
    (meaning (body-of closure)
      (extend-table
        (new-entry
          (formals-of closure) vals)
        (table-of closure)))))
```

This is a complicated function and it deserves an example.	In the following
	    closure is (((((u v w)
	           (1 2 3))
	        ((x y z)
	         (4 5 6)))
	      (x y)
	      (cons z x))
	and
	    vals is ((a b c) (d e f)).

What will be the new arguments for meaning?	The new *e* for meaning will be (cons z x) and the new *table* for meaning will be
	    (((x y)
	      ((a b c) (d e f)))
	     ((u v w)
	      (1 2 3))
	     ((x y z)
	      (4 5 6))).

What is the meaning of (cons z x) where	The same as
z is 6, and	(meaning e *table*) .
x is (a b c)	where
	e is (cons z x), and
	table is (((x y)
	((a b c) (d e f)))
	((u v w)
	(1 2 3))
	((x y z)
	(4 5 6))).

Let's find the meaning of all the arguments.	In order to do this we must find both
What is	(meaning e *table*)
(evlis *args* *table*),	where
where	e is z,
args is (z x),	and
and	(meaning e *table*)
table is (((x y)	where
((a b c) (d e f)))	e is x.
((u v w)	
(1 2 3))	
((x y z)	
(4 5 6)))	

What is the (meaning e *table*) where	6, by using *identifier.
e is z	

What is (meaning e *table*) where	(a b c), by using *identifier.
e is x	

So, what is the result of evlis	(6 (a b c)), because evlis returns a list of the meanings.

What is (meaning e *table*) where	(primitive cons), by using *identifier.
e is cons.	

We are now ready to (apply *fun vals*) where
  fun is (primitive cons), and
  vals is (6 (a b c)).
Which path will we take?
	The apply-primitive path.

Which cond-line is chosen for
  (apply-primitive *name vals*)
where
  name is cons, and
  vals is (6 (a b c))
	The third:
	  ((eq? *name* (**quote** cons))
	  (cons (first *vals*) (second *vals*))).

What is (first *vals*) where *vals* is (6 (a b c))	6

What is (second *vals*) where *vals* is (6 (a b c))	(a b c).

What is (cons *alpha beta*) where
  alpha is 6, and
  beta is (a b c)
	(6 a b c).

What is
  ((**lambda** (*u v*)
    (**lambda** (*b*)
      (**cond**
        (*b u*)
        (t *v*))))
   alpha
   beta)
where
  alpha is 6, and
  beta is (a b c)
	It is a shadow of the list (6 a b c).

Why?	Because we can define cons by

```
(define cons
  (lambda (u v)
    (lambda (b)
      (cond
        (b u)
        (t v)))))
```

How does this work?	Well, let's step through a simple example.

```
(define lunch (cons x y))
```

where
   x is **apple**, and
   y is ( )

The function lunch takes an argument, *b*. If *b* is true, the car, *x*, is returned (i.e., **apple**). If *b* is false, the cdr, *y*, is returned (i.e., ( )).

Define car and cdr for lists using this representation.

```
(define car
  (lambda (l)
    (l t)))
```

```
(define cdr
  (lambda (l)
    (l nil)))
```

What is (car lunch)	**apple**.

What is (cdr lunch)	( ).

Is that what we wanted?	Yes.

Can we cons lunch onto lunch?	Yes, (cons lunch lunch).

What is the Value of All of This?

How many cond-lines do we really need in apply-primitive	Just two.

Which ones are they?	The eq? and the atom? cond-lines. We just eliminated car, cdr, and cons, and in Chapter 7 we showed that numbers could be represented with lists. Can you recall when not and null? were defined?

But what about (**define** ...)	It isn't needed either because recursion can be obtained with the Y-combinator.

Does that mean we can run the interpreter on the interpreter if we do the transformation with the Y-combinator?	Yes, but don't bother.

t	Yes, it's time for a banquet.

"Koot's Banquet"

Is this

    (Y (**lambda** (∞)

        (cons (sub1 1) ∞)))

the same as this

    (Y (**lambda** (∞)

        (cons 0 ∞)))

Try it with

```
(define cons
    (lambda (u v)
        (lambda (b)
            (cond
                (b u)
                (t v)))))
```

Exercises

For these exercises,

> $e1$ is ((lambda (x)
>   (cond
>   ((atom? x) (quote done))
>   ((null? x) (quote almost))
>   (t (quote never))))
>   (quote _____)),
>
> $e2$ is (((lambda (x y)
>   (lambda (u)
>   (cond
>   (u x)
>   (t y))))
>   1 ( ))
>   nil),
>
> $e3$ is ((lambda (x)
>   ((lambda (x)
>   (add1 x))
>   (add1 4)))
>   6),
>
> $e4$ is (3 (quote a) (quote b)),
>
> $e5$ is (lambda (lat) (cons (quote lat) lat)),
>
> $e6$ is (lambda (lat (lyst)) a (quote b)).

10.1 Make up examples for e and step through (value e). The examples should cover truth values, numbers, and quoted S-expressions.

10.2 Make up some S-expressions, plug them into the _____ of $e1$, and step through the application of (value $e1$).

10.3 Step through the application of (value $e2$). How many closures are produced during the application?

10.4 Consider the expression *e3*. What do you expect to be the value of *e3*? Which of the three x's are "related"? Verify your answers by stepping through (value *e3*). Observe to which x we add one.

10.5 Design a representation for closures and primitives such that the tags (i.e., primitive and non-primitive) at the beginning of the lists become unnecessary. Rewrite the functions that are knowledgeable of the structures. Step through (value *e3*) with the new interpreter.

10.6 Just as the table for predetermined identifiers, initial-table, all tables in our interpreter can be represented as functions. Then, the function extend-table is changed to:

```
(define extend-table
  (lambda (entry table)
    (lambda (name)
      (cond
        ((member? name (first entry))
         (pick (index name (first entry))
           (second entry)))
        (t (table name))))))
```

(For pick see Chapter 4; for index see Exercise 4.5.) What else has to be changed to make the interpreter work? Make the least number of changes. Make up an application of value to your favorite expression and step through it to make sure you understand the new representation. Hint: Look at all the places where tables are used to find out where changes have to be made.

10.7 Write the function ∗lambda? which checks whether an S-expression is really a representation of a lambda-function.

Example: (∗lambda? *e5*) is true,
               (∗lambda? *e6*) is false,
               (∗lambda? *e2*) is false.
Also write the functions ∗quote? and ∗cond? which do the same for quote- and cond-expressions.

10.8 Non-primitive functions are represented by lists in our interpreter. An alternative is to use functions to represent functions. For this we change ∗lambda to:

```
(define *lambda
  (lambda (e table)
    (build
      (quote non-primitive)
      (lambda (vals)
        (meaning (body-of e)
          (extend-table
            (new-entry (formals-of e) vals)
            table))))))
```

How do we have to change apply-closure to make this representation work? Do we need to change anything else? Walk through the application (value *e2*) to become familiar with this new representation.

10.9 Primitive functions are built repeatedly while finding the value of an expression. To see this, step through the application (value *e3*) and count how often the primitive for **add1** is built. However, consider the following table for predetermined identifiers:

```
(define initial-table
  ((lambda (add1)
     (lambda (name)
       (cond
         ((eq? name (quote t)) t)
         ((eq? name (quote nil)) nil)
         ((eq? name (quote add1)) add1)
         (t (build (quote primitive) name)))))
   (build (quote primitive) add1)))
```

Using this initial-table, how does the count change? Generalize this approach to include all primitives.

10.10 In Exercise 2.4 we introduced the (**if** ...)-form. We saw that (**if** ...) and (**cond** ...) are interchangeable. If we replace the function ∗cond by ∗if where

```
(define ∗if
  (lambda (e table)
    (if (meaning (test-pt e) table)
        (meaning (then-pt e) table)
        (meaning (else-pt e) table))))
```

we can almost evaluate functions containing (**if** ...). What other changes do we have to make? Make the changes. Take all the examples from this chapter that contain a (**cond** ...), rewrite them with (**if** ...), and step through the modified interpreter. Do the same for *e1* and *e2*.

Welcome to the Show

You have reached the end of your introduction to Lisp and recursion. Are you now ready to tackle a major programming problem in Lisp? Programming in Lisp requires two kinds of knowledge: understanding the nature of symbolic programming and recursion, and discovering the lexicon, features, and idiosyncrasies of a particular Lisp implementation. The first of these is the more difficult intellectual task. If you understand the material in this book, you have mastered that challenge. In any case, it would be well worth your time to develop a fuller understanding of all the capabilities in Lisp—this requires getting access to a running Lisp system and mastering those idiosyncrasies. If you want to understand Lisp in greater depth, the first, second, and fourth references are good choices for further reading. Abelson, Sussman, and Sussman [1] develops the concepts required for building large programs. Dybvig [2] describes Scheme, the Lisp-descendant used throughout this book. Steele [4] is the reference manual for Common Lisp, an increasingly popular dialect. Reading these books will give you some of the flavor of the features found in complete Lisp systems. We recommend Suppes [5] to the reader who wants to explore symbolic manipulation in a non-programming context, and Hofstadter [3] to the reader who wants to examine the place of recursion in the context of human thought.

References

[1] Abelson, H. & Sussman, G. J., with J. Sussman. *Structure and Interpretation of Computer Programs.* The MIT Press, Cambridge, Massachusetts, 1985.

[2] Dybvig, R. K. *The Scheme Programming Language.* Prentice-Hall Inc., Englewood Cliffs, New Jersey, 1987.

[3] Hofstadter, D. R. *Gödel, Escher, Bach: an Eternal Golden Braid.* Basic Books, Inc., New York, 1979.

[4] Steele, G. L., Jr. *Common Lisp: The Language.* Digital Press, Bedford, Massachusetts, 1984.

[5] Suppes, P. *Introduction to Logic.* Van Nostrand Co., Princeton, New Jersey, 1957.

Index